Cambridg

C000193784

BEST
pubs

Compiled and edited by
Ted Bruning

Photographs by
**Ted Bruning, Mick Slaughter, Rob
Lampard, and Nigel Frost**

COUNTY LIFE
PUBLISHING

Published by County Life Publishing
33 Jacobs Close
Potton
Bedfordshire SG19 2SG

Copyright © County Life Publishing 2009

ISBN: 978-0-9562973-0-3

A catalogue record for this book is available from the British Library

The publishers have made every effort to ensure the accuracy of information in this book at time of going to press. However they cannot accept responsibility for any loss, injury or inconvenience resulting from the use of information contained in this guide.

Publisher: Nigel Frost
Cover design: John Simpson

Cover picture: John Barleycorn, Duxford

Contents

Introduction

These are tough times for Britain's pubs. Even before the recession hit they were already feeling the effects of the smoking ban, competition from home entertainment, and soaring overheads. To make things worse, local authorities have been imposing more and more onerous conditions on their licences, while a Chancellor in thrall to a medical lobby reliant on some very dodgy statistics went apparently barmy and started merrily ramping up beer duty – by 17% in 2008 alone! Not surprising, then, that Britain is currently haemorrhaging pubs at a rate of more than 30 a week.

But the good news for you, the public, is that the pub trade is fighting back by constantly improving its standards in every department. Licensees know, simply from counting their takings, that for more and more of us a trip to the pub is

Royak Oak, Barrington

becoming an occasional treat rather than an everyday indulgence. And they know – or the smart ones do, at any rate – that we are no longer prepared to put up with sour beer, undrinkable wine, mass-produced food, tired décor, so-called beer gardens that are actually no more than a couple of picnic tables in the car park, and loos that are frankly unspeakable.

The smart ones are also making provision for customers with disabilities, especially those confined to wheelchairs. One of the glories of the Great British Pub is that it is, or should be, a haven for everyone from princes down, and that must include people with disabilities. Many pubs, of course, have difficulty making proper provision for wheelchair users – split levels, frequent steps, narrow gangways and sudden corners are unavoidable features of ancient buildings. Many that could, though, use this as an excuse for not making the investment. Which in the long term is a false economy, for there are hundreds of thousands of wheelchair users out there who would dearly love to make more use of pubs if only they could... and they have millions of friends who'll come with them!

This new guide recognises, rewards, and directs you to some of the pubs that have gone the extra mile to make your visit the treat you expect and deserve. Of course, there'll be many pubs that deserve to be listed that, through my own ignorance, I have left out. Everybody has their own favourite, and you can help put my omissions right and give justice to your favourite licensee by sending back to me the information detailed on page 114 of this book. Every pub nominated by readers will be inspected and considered for inclusion in the next edition.

Unfortunate omissions notwithstanding, in these pages you'll find all sorts of pubs – village inns, backstreet locals, family-friendly pubs, foodie heavens, pubs with letting rooms, real ale enthusiasts' Meccas – something for everyone, in fact. What they have in common is licensees who genuinely love their calling and get their greatest satisfaction from satisfying you.

So reintroduce yourself to the simple pleasures of turning off the TV (and however big a screen or however many cable and satellite channels you've got, there's never anything any good on) and strolling down to the pub instead . Have a slap-up meal or just a couple of drinks. Go with friends, or go on your own and make new friends. Have a game of pool, or darts, or dominoes, or just enjoy the conversation. Actually get to know your neighbours, and find out what's going on in your town or village.

And when you get there, tell them Ted sent you!

Ted Bruning
April 2009.

Beer Quality

Few things in everyday life are more of a disappointment than bad beer. You've made the decision not to stay in but to go to the pub, perhaps for lunch with friends or family, perhaps just for a casual drink. By the time you get there you're really looking forward to a lovely, cool, clean, refreshing pint of sparkling ale. You arrive at the bar. You scan the handpumps to see what's on offer. You order. You pay. You raise the glass to your lips... and you get a mouthful of brackish, stale, oxidised, vinegary mush.

Bad beer was one of the reasons why so many people turned to keg ales in the 1960s and then lagers in the 1970s and '80s. Bad ale is one of the reasons why to this day two out of every three pints sold in our pubs is not traditional British beer but foreign-derived (although almost all British-brewed) lager.

Fortunately, the quality of Britain's beer is getting better and better... and not just because there are more and more local brewers dedicated to producing top-class real ales, but because licensees are getting better and better at keeping and serving it properly.

And cask-conditioned beer takes some keeping. It's alive, for one thing – every barrel of real ale contains a thriving population of living yeast cells, all browsing gently on

THE SIGN OF A GREAT PINT
INDEPENDENTLY INSPECTED

the malt sugars to produce the natural CO_2 that gives your pint its sparkle. Unfiltered and unpasteurised, once it's tapped it becomes vulnerable to infection by airborne micro-organisms that can only be kept at bay by rigorous cleanliness all the way from cellar to glass. It oxidises, too: as pints are drawn off, air is allowed into the barrel – and that means it has a short shelf-life, three or four days at most from the moment it's tapped. So, proper stock rotation and a brisk rate of sale are vital if customers are to enjoy their pints fresh. And to be refreshing, it needs to be cool. Not necessarily cold, but cool – which means properly equipped cellars.

In recent years, brewers and pub operators have invested millions both in their pub cellars and in training their licensees. And for the last 12 years an independent organisation has been working alongside them to make sure that every pint you get is at its best.

That organisation is Cask Marque, whose distinctive handpump logo on a wall-plaque proudly displayed at the front door of accredited pubs is an increasingly familiar sight to Britain's beer lovers.

They may not know that it means the pub is inspected twice a year by one of 44 experienced assessors, who methodically check the temperature, clarity, aroma and flavour of every real ale on offer on the bar.

But they do know that it means they can be sure of a quality pint.

Cask Marque was founded in 1997 by Paul Nunny, a former director of legendary Suffolk brewer Adnams, to raise standards in the keeping and serving of cask-conditioned beer. Since then it has grown and grown, and its coveted plaque is now on display at over 5,000 pubs the length and breadth of Britain.

Not all licensees have signed up for Cask Marque accreditation. For one thing, it's expensive. And there's always the fear of failing to pass the inspection. Then there are landlords who feel their reputation is such that they don't need it confirmed independently. So although the absence of a Cask Marque plaque at the pub door doesn't necessarily mean the beer isn't up to scratch, wherever you do see one you know you're in for a well-kept, well-served pint.

That's why we've decided to mark all the Cask Marque-accredited pubs in this guide with a miniature version of the organisation's logo. Because the Cask Marque plaque is the sure sign of a good pint.

Abington Pigotts

Pig & Abbot
High St SG8 0SD
Tel 01763 853515
www.pigandabbot.
co.uk

One thing Cambridge-shire folk do well is fight to save their village pubs. Quite a number of pubs in the county have been rescued from closure by villagers clubbing together either to oppose change of use permission or to raise the purchase price or both; and the villagers of Abington Piggots were among the pioneers of this robust form of self-help.

The pub's rather elegant three-bay early Georgian façade with its sash windows and pedimented door-frame conceals an even older building that was probably originally built as a dower house for the Piggott family, lords of the manor here since 1426. By 1835 it had become the village pub, possibly taking advantage of

AT A GLANCE
Opening times: 12-3, 6-11 Mon-Fri; 11-11 Sat; 12-11 Sun. Food service: 12-2, 6-9 Mon-Fri; 12-2.30, 6-9 Sat-Sun. Mains/specials £4.95-£10.95. Real ales: Adnams Bitter, Fuller's London Pride; two guests. Small car park; patio; beer garden. Children and dogs welcome.

the 1830 Beer Act that allowed householders to sell ale (but not spirits) without a justice's licence.

But Abington Piggotts is a tiny village and quite remote, approached only by a single-track lane; and by the mid-1990s the owner had decided that the Darby & Joan, as it then was, was no longer viable, so he closed it and applied for permission to change its use to a private dwelling. The application was vigorously and successfully opposed by the villagers, who also raised enough money – nearly £200,000 – to buy and refurbish it. For a few years they ran it themselves, letting it out to a tenant and advising other villagers in the same situation on how to go about matters.

Now the pub has been sold and is run as a regular free house; but the villagers still have a fierce pride in their achievement and flock to it in droves. And not just because it was once their property, either, but because it's such a cosy, comfortable, pub with its big L-shaped bar, its two fireplaces, its natural-gold oak beams, its plush upholstery, its deep armchairs, and its classy dining-room, that there's really no reason to stay at home.

Arrington

Hardwicke Arms

Old North Rd SG8 0AH
Tel 01223 208802
www.hardwickearmshotel.
co.uk

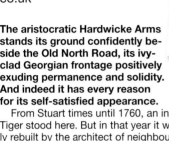

The aristocratic Hardwicke Arms stands its ground confidently beside the Old North Road, its ivy-clad Georgian frontage positively exuding permanence and solidity. And indeed it has every reason for its self-satisfied appearance.

From Stuart times until 1760, an inn named the Tiger stood here. But in that year it was completely rebuilt by the architect of neighbouring Wimpole Hall, none other than Sir John Soane, and renamed after the Hardwicke family who owned the Hall. And as if that wasn't blue-blooded enough, the inn was taken over by a former butler of the Hardwickes' and was used as overflow accommodation for Wimpole's guests and their servants, guaranteeing some very plummy accents indeed in the coffee-room.

The main business, though, was the coach trade; and when that collapsed it left the Hardwicke Arms stranded. Over the years bits and pieces of what had been a very grand establishment indeed were sold to stave off bankruptcy – the coach-house is today the village hall; the orchard is a nursing home; six houses stand on the old coach yard; there are more houses on the former paddock across the road – but the recession of the early 1990s proved too much, and in October 1991 it closed.

It stood empty until May 1993 when at last it was bought, restored, and reopened, and today it has regained much of the affluent, aristocratic mien of old. The panelled dining room is elegance itself, save for the incongruous huge fireplace which was originally Soane's revolutionary central heating system from which hot-air ducts radiated to heat the bedrooms above. There's a smaller dining room, also panelled, with a more modest stone fireplace; the main bar is plush but not too formal, and has up to four cask beers including Greene King IPA and guests; beyond that is a second much smaller bar; and finally a large functions room.

AT A GLANCE
Opening times: 11.30-11 all week. Food service: 12-2.15, 6.30-9.30 Mon-Sat; 12-9 Sun. Mains/specials £9.95-£15. Wifi/internet access. 12 letting rooms, £50 single, £70 double. Car park. Small garden. Children welcome.

Barrington

Royal Oak
The Green CB22 7RZ Tel 01223 870971 www.royaloak.uk.net

The Royal Oak is one of those annoying pubs that ought to be dripping with history. Its low thatched roof and stout upright timbers ought to have sheltered Elizabeth I, Oliver

Cromwell, Dick Turpin and all the other habitués of English inns of this character and vintage; but if they ever came, they never signed the visitors' book.

Don't be put off, though: the Royal Oak – which overlooks England's biggest village green at 22 acres – is genuinely ancient. Perhaps not quite as ancient as it claims – there are very, very few domestic buildings of the 13th century about the place these days – but certainly pre-Tudor. Its two bays, central recess, and jettied upper floors reveal it as being a "hall house", and therefore the dwelling of of a prosperous yeoman and his family from the late 15th century; it has been a pub (it seems never to have been an inn) since at least the 1850s, and in 1968 became the last in a village that once had seven.

Today it still serves local drinkers with a selection that includes Young's Bitter, Adnams Bitter, and Potton Brewery Shannon IPA, in a heavily beamed bar with quarry-tiled floor and a tiny little snug up some steps off to one side. But it makes its living mainly as a dining pub. To get to the dining room you have to, as the saying has it, "duck or grouse", for access from the bar is actually through the former fireplace, a huge and ancient construction of brick (probably inserted in Stuart times, before which the central bay would have been a great hall open to the roof) on whose low lintels rests an immovable mass of masonry. That dining rules here is attested by the fact that beyond the first dining room there lies a second, and beyond that a conservatory used for dining.

AT A GLANCE
Opening times: 12-2.30, 6-11 Mon-Sat; 12-3, 6.30-10.30 Sun. Food service: 12-2, 6-9.30 Mon-Sat; 12-2.30, 7-9 Sun. Mains £10.65 -£22.75. Light lunches Mon-Sat £7. Car park. Children welcome; dogs allowed in bar.

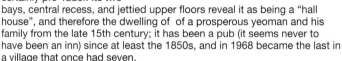

Cambridge

Cambridge Blue
85 Gwydir St CB1 2LG
Tel 01223 361382

The large district of narrow Victorian terraced streets to the south of the historic city centre is not unusual in the number of corner locals with which its developers originally endowed it; what is unusual is how many have survived. Even more unusual is the proportion of them that have built their reputations on the quality and variety of cask ales they serve:

so much so that among the cognoscenti this part of Cambridge is known as "the Beer Quarter".

Among the best-known is the Cambridge Blue (the Dew Drop until the 1980s), an unassuming little late Victorian pub halfway down a long street of small but distinctly gentrified terraces. It may not look much from the outside, but step inside and the first thing you see is a chiller cabinet full of mind-blowingly strong Belgian bottled beers. Once at the bar you're faced with a thicket of hand-pumps from which up to 14 real ales are dispensed. Only two of them – Woodforde's Wherry and Cambridge Blue Dew Drop (Nethergate 3.9 specially badged for the pub) are regulars. The rest come from mainly from micro-breweries from all over Britain: the rows of pumpclips decorating the walls of the U-shaped bar are a reminder of many succulent offerings from the past. And on top of that, the pub also stocks up to three traditional ciders and even that rarity of rarities, a perry.

AT A GLANCE

Opening hours: 12-2.30, 5-11 Mon-Wed; 12-11 Thurs-Sat; 12-10.30 Sun. Food service 12-2, 6-9 Mon-Fri; 12-4, 6-9 Sat-Sun. Mains £7-£10; smaller portions £5-£8. Children in garden and con-servatory to 9pm. Dogs allowed. Parking difficult.

Unusually in such a location, there's a lovely big garden at the back which has, so the staff say, more tables and chairs than the bar does!

Champion of the Thames
68 King St CB1 1LN
Tel 01223 352043

Not many city centres can boast a charming survival from the past like the tiny Champion of the Thames. Origi-nally a pair of 18th-century cottages, it was knocked into one and turned into pub about 150 years ago – probably between 1830 and 1869, when the Beer Act allowed any householder to sell beer without a licence. The two bars are as olde-worlde as you could hope for: wood-panelled walls; open fires; low ceilings; wooden benches and tables and

AT A GLANCE

Opening hours: 12-11 Sun-Thurs; 11-11 Fri-Sat. Children admit-ted until early evening; well-behaved dogs welcome.

lino flooring in the public bar; bottle-green leather upholstery and baize-covered card tables and bare floorboards in the snug. The name supposedly derives from the days before street numbering, when one of the cottages was home to a former oarsman to whom letters would be addressed simply as "the champion of the Thames"; the theme is maintained with a display of old sculls and other rowing memorabilia.

The real ales are from Greene King with a couple of guests. There's a small courtyard for smokers, but the Champion doesn't serve food.

Eagle

8 Bene't St CB2 3QN
Tel 01223 505020

Despite its unimpressive-to-the-point-of-invisible street frontage, the Eagle is probably Cambridge's oldest pub, with parts of the building dating back to the 1600s when it was a posting-house called the Eagle & Child. In the early 19th century the courtyard galleries acquired their elegant wrought-iron balconies, once a common feature of well-heeled inns but now a great rarity; and in the later Victorian years the bar at the back of the courtyard was added, to gain fame as the RAF Bar owing to the habit of World War II airmen (both British and American) of writing their names on the ceiling with smoke from their cigarette lighters. Sobering to wonder how many of those names belong to young men who never came home.

After the war, the Eagle became a popular lunchtime venue for researchers from the (then) nearby Cavendish Laboratories, among them James Watson and Bernard Crick. At lunchtime on 28th February 1953 an overexcited Crick announced to fellow-diners, most of whom must have wondered what he was talking about, that he and Watson had discovered the secret of life itself. He wasn't exaggerating: the pair had just discovered the DNA double helix. But in his memoirs, Watson described Crick's announcement as "bragging" and "somewhat immodest".

AT A GLANCE

Opening times: 11-11 Mon-Sat; 12-11 Sun. Food service: 12-10. Mains £7-£12. Children welcome until early evening. Parking difficult.

The Eagle is a big, rambling pub with four or possibly five (depending on how you classify them) bars and snugs, each with its own character. The dining room overlooking Bene't street, with its Georgian panelling and fireplace and 18th-century fashion prints, has the atmosphere of a gentleman's club or the senior common room of a particularly lofty colllege. Don't be fooled, though. In the late 1980s the freeholder, Corpus Christi, closed the pub in order to turn it into student accommodation. This act of sacrilege was bitterly opposed; and eventually the college relented and leased the Eagle to Greene King, which reopened it in 1992 after a thorough restoration. The project included the creation from scratch of this elegant early Georgian salon.

Elm Tree

Orchard St CB1 1JS
Tel 01223 363005

Behind the police station and within spitting distance of Parker's Piece is a maze of charming little lanes of gentrified terraces, including the aptly named Paradise Street and Eden Street. On the corner of Eden Street and Orchard Street you'll find the Elm Tree, which thanks to its unusual ownership arrangements has developed a reputation as one of the city's premier real ale pubs. It actually belongs to Charles Wells of Bedford, whose range you'll find on handpump; but it's leased to Banks & Taylor of Shefford, whose beers you will therefore also see on the bar along with up to four guest ales, at least one farmhouse cider, and a selection of around 65 strong bottled beers from Belgium. For Guinness drinkers, the Elm Tree offers a rare opportunity to try an alternative: Charles Wells's excellent Bowman Stout is an export brand served (mysteriously, given its excellence) in only a tiny handful of pubs in the UK.

The pub itself was converted from three cottages only in the 1930s and consists

of a single long split-level bar, with bare floorboards and wooden chairs at one end and carpets and upholstery at the other. It's busy with beer-related bric-a-brac including enamel advertisements, stoneware crocks, German steins, and an impressive collection of beer bottles, some dating back to the 1960s.

The Elm Tree doesn't do food, although you can buy a bowl of olives or a plate of savoury nibbles for £5.

Free Press
Prospect Row CB1 1DU
Tel 01223 368337

 A Cambridge legend, the Free Press was one of the two city pubs – the other was the Cambridge Blue – that banned tobacco years before the Government did. Tobacco is still banned on the premises, even in the pub's walled garden. Mobiles are banned, too. Like the surrounding streets, the Free Press is cottage-style and may have been built as one, probably in the 1850s or '60s. It was always called the Free Press but was never, as legend has it, a newspaper office, although a single edition of a free newspaper was supposedly put together here in the 1960s. Its name recalls a radical newspaper of the 1830s and is a reminder that left-wing politics were just as much a feature of the mid-19th century as the mid-20th.

Its two bars are as traditional and homely as you could wish, all low ceilings and settles; and one end of the public bar was partitioned off – perhaps in the 1890s, when there was a mania for privacy, or possibly, since it once had its own street door, as a bottle and jug – to form a tiny snug with room for only a single table (although 61 undergraduates somehow heaped themselves into it one memorable evening in 1978).

The interesting thing about the interior, though, is that however time-honoured it looks, it's actually comparatively new: the pub was gutted in 1975 to make way for a redevelopment that never took place, and the original fixtures and fittings had to be painstakingly reassembled.

Real ales are from the Greene King range, plus a guest or two.

Green Dragon
5 Water St CB4 1NZ
Tel 01223 505035

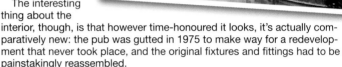

Licensed since 1630, the Green Dragon with its pink-washed jettied front claims to be Cambridge's second oldest inn after the Eagle, allegedly numbering Oliver Cromwell among its guests. It's certainly one of the best-located, just across Water Street from a foot (and, of course, bicycle) bridge over the Cam where in days of yore a ferry plied to and fro.

Inside, attempts by owner Greene King to open up the interior have been undermined by an enormous (and still operative) brick-built inglenook fireplace that effectively divides the low-ceilinged and only moderately oak-beamed bar in two. The skeleton of an original stud wall, marking the former existence of a third bar or parlour, subdivides the interior still further; so although you could technically call it open-plan it still has plenty of cosy, intimate little nooks and corners for those inclined to privacy.

Very much a local, the Green Dragon and its regulars have raised a fearsome amount for charity by many and devious means such as a second-hand book exchange. It's also a nest of avid cribbage-players, who have two tables reserved at weekends. But with the riverside footpath (and, of course, cycle path) running virtually past its front door, it also attracts plenty of passing trade. The well-priced Greene King and guest ales (XX Mild at just £2.20 a pint) and the varied food offering including a wide range of locally-made sausages keep the pub bustling.

Kingston Arms
33 Kingston St
CB1 2NU
Tel 01223
319414

 Another of the wonderful little street-corner pubs that have survived so well in the gentrified Victorian terraces of south Cambridge (how gentrified? Well, the workshop opposite makes violin bows), the Kingston Arms may look olde-worlde from outside (despite the bright blue frontage!), but inside it's nothing of the sort. Check the shocking blue-green upholstery on the benches in the big L-shaped bar and the free internet access – but check also the open fire that says traditional comfort and cosiness. The garden's cosy too – it's heated and even boasts a sofa!

And check, also, a range of cask beers that includes three Champion Beer of Britain competition winners (Crouch Vale Brewers Gold, Oakham JHB, and Timothy Taylor Landlord) as well as a dark mild and a cask stout as regulars, along with five guest ales and a farmhouse cider.

The guest principle extends beyond the beers to the menu, with changing guest sausages from a local butcher and, for the fat-conscious, ostrich steaks.

Children are welcome during food service, and well-controlled dogs are always welcome.

Live & Let Live
40 Mawson Rd CB1 2EA
Tel 01223 460261

The Holy Trinity of legendary south Cambridge real ale pubs is made up of the Cambridge Blue, the Free Press, and the Live & Let Live. Others have more recently taken up the burden of purveying a terrific range of microbrewery beers to a grateful public, but these three were at it 20 years ago and more, right back to the days when the country was awash with keg beer and choice was – well, not much to choose from.

As pleasantly scruffy and lived-in as the favourite trainers you just can't throw away (although,perhaps, not as smelly), the Live & Let Live occupies the middle of a terraced row of

1870 or thereabouts. Its single long, narrow bar has matchboarded walls, fixed wooden benches, bare floorboards, a cheery woodburning stove and, somewhat anachronistically, a beamed ceiling. Just the right surroundings, in fact, for a beer range that boasts seven handpumps (Everard's Tiger, Nethergate Umbel Ale and Oakham Inferno are the regulars), a rare draught Belgian beer, a farmhouse cider, and a choice of 40 bottled Belgian beers. There's also a tiny snug at the back for those truly intimate evenings.

Old Spring
1 Ferry Path, Chesterton Rd
CB4 1HB
Tel 01223 309796

Anyone who last visited this tiny terraced early Victorian pub 15 years ago would have quite a shock if they walked in now. A succession of alterations and extensions has transformed what used to be a traditional and rather dark little local – gas-lit, in fact – just a stone's throw from the Cam into what can only be described as an ultra-chic bar-brasserie. A sunny conservatory leads through to a charming walled courtyard, and also fills the pale green and yellow painted main bar with light and air. An extension off to one side is a warmer and cosier soft area. The only signs of antiquity are a functioning bare brick fireplace and what look like the original floor-boards, which are somewhat battered and buckled.

A hugely popular dining pub, the Old Spring is also well-used by drinkers and keeps the Greene King range plus a guest ale. Unusually for this part of town, the Old Spring has its own car park: the access is actually on Chesterton Road, but it's a bit blink-and-you'll miss it.

Salisbury Arms

76 Tenison Rd CB1 2DW
Tel 01223 576363

Here's a pub with a past. Handy for the city's railway station, it was actually built as a small hotel and originally had a floor of letting rooms at the back. Then in 1976 it was the first pub to be bought by CAMRA Investments, the Campaign for Real Ale's short-lived attempt at showing the big brewers how proper pubs ought to be run. CAMRA's major contribution was to turn the hotel section into a sort of great hall by ripping out the floor completely, creating a high-ceilinged area rather like a Victorian concert room that now has a false minstrels' gallery, home to a pair of mannequins posed at a table. There's a third mannequin, riding a bike, hanging from the rafters alongside a hop pocket that may or may not be real.

AT A GLANCE
Opening hours:
12-2.30, 5-11
Mon-Thurs;
12-2.30 5-12 Fri;
12-2.30, 6-12 Sat;
12-2.30, 7-10.30
Sun. Food service: 12-2, 5.30-10
Mon-Fri; Mains
£4-£7.25. No
food Sat-Sun, but
bring a takeaway
and the pub will
provide crockery
and cutlery.

The days of CAMRA Investments are long gone, but the spirit lives on here. Although a Charles Wells tied house, the Salisbury has six guest ales and an organic farmhouse cider from Crone's of Norfolk. It is also surely the only pub in Cambridge where you can play Ring the Bull, a fiendishly difficult variant on quoits.

St Radegund

129 King Street CB1 1LD
Tel 01223 311749
www.radegund.co.uk

Certainly Cambridge's smallest and arguably one of its most famous pubs, the St Radegund is peculiar in any number of ways.

The most obvious is its size: it's a roughly equilateral triangle (which is peculiar enough in itself) of about 18ft per side. That gives it an area of... well, half the base times the height; you can work it out for yourself. But it doesn't take that many undergraduates to fill it to bursting. And actually, it wasn't always so small. Until the 1960s it had a vaults or cellar bar that was bigger than the ground floor; old photographs show the basement's little fanlights at pavement level.

Then there's the name. St Radegund was a 6th-century German princess who was captured at the age of 11 in the Frankish invasion of Thuringia, and at the age of 18 was forcibly married to her captor, King Clothaire. Her piety and austerity drove him to distraction, however, and eventually she escaped his clutches, founding an order of nuns in Poitiers when he died. Her connection with Cambridge? Jesus College, just round the corner from the pub, was built on the site of a convent of her order, and she remains the Collage's patron saint.

What next? There's the wall of shame, where your name is recorded for ever should you commit the sin of being unable to finish your drink when time is called, and the raincheck tree, where you can leave a ticket to say you've put a drink in the pipe for a friend.

Then there's the pub's sporting regulars: small it may be, but the St Radegund supports a touring cricket team, a rowing club, and the famous Hash House Harriers, described as a running club with a drink problem. "The Hash" still occasionally re-enacts the King Street Run, in which new undergraduates were required to drink a pint in each of King Street's 14 pubs against the clock and without "peeing or puking". There are only five now, so it's easier.

Finally there's the ownership. Next door is a row of six almshouses which were built in 1880 to replace an older set that were beyond repair. The building left an odd-shaped scrap of land at one end, which the trustees filled by building the pub. They own it still.

One last thing: the St Radegund is the only genuine free house in the city centre and the cask beers – Milton sackcloth, Fuller's London pride, and up to three guests – are outstanding.

Coton

Plough
High St CB3 7PL. Tel 01954 267251. www.theploughcoton.co.uk

Not many villages this small have managed to hang on to their pubs: the fact that Coton has is the result of a metamorphosis so fundamental as to be almost shocking.
From the outside, the Plough is an unremarkable and rather dumpy building of perhaps the early 19th century, with a nice red-tiled roof and a rather incongruous glass porch. Only the colour-scheme –

the brickwork, which one feels should be a mellow red, is painted a pale putty colour while the window frames, which should be white, are Farrow & Ball green – gives a hint of anything unusual going on.

Step inside, and you are whisked away from the countryside and into a chic and very modern urban restaurant, all Mediterranean-style floor tiles, pale woodwork, and leather-upholstered chairs and benches – a Pizza Express with real ale, you might call it. (For the record, the real ales are Greene King IPA, Timothy Taylor Landlord, and Adnams Broadside). For although villagers do still pop in for a pint and a gossip – and are made very welcome – this is a dining destination pub par excellence. The range of food on offer, both in the bar and in the elegant dining room, is astonishing: tapas; stone-baked pizzas fresh from the pub's own oven; fish

and chips; vegetarian gnocchi; enormous steaks. The pub opens early for coffee and pastries, too, and despite its being three miles from the centre of Cambridge, there's a steady trickle of custom.

The car park is, perhaps unsurprisingly, one of the largest I have ever seen at any pub, and is always full. And indeed the pub's outdoor areas work as hard for their living as the bar and dining room do: there's a pleasant patio with tables and chairs for al fresco dining including hog roasts and barbecues in summer; a huge garden with elaborate play equipment; and a field that hosts events such as farmer's markets and jazz picnics. So: not a traditional village pub, but perhaps one that shows a way that others will follow.

Croydon

Queen Adelaide
High St SG8 0DN Tel 01223 208278 www.queen-adelaide.co.uk

Strange thing, fate. In the Middle Ages, Croydon was merely a hamlet in the parish of Clopton. Then in the 16th century Clopton ran out of steam and was abandoned: today it's a well-known deserted site and gives its name to a long cross-country walk.

Croydon, on the other hand, put on a growth spurt in the early 19th century and is today a thriving village in its own right, with the Queen Adelaide at its geographical as well as metaphorical heart. (The name, by the way, is a good clue to the pub's date of origin: Adelaide was the wife of William IV, who reigned from 1830-1837 and gave his name to a fair few pubs in the county).

Originally, as you can see just by looking, the Queen Adelaide was a tiny pub – not much more than a cottage, really. But in the 1970s it was briefly turned into a restaurant, and the work of extending it began. Today, as well as the big extension at the front, there's a sunny conservatory and a decked platform for al fresco drinking and dining on sunny days; while at the back there's the huge and well-equipped garden and play area for which the Queen Adelaide is well-known in the district.

In summer this garden is packed with families and often hosts outdoor events. But don't neglect the pub in winter, either: inside it's spacious and comfortable with a big fireplace containing a cheery woodburning stove, and plenty of deep sofas for those who like to relax in style. The food is no-nonsense British, with home-made pies a speciality; the beers are Greene King IPA plus up to three guests.

Dullingham

Boot
18 Brinkley Rd CB8 9UW
Tel 01638 507327

Dullingham has a posher pub, the kings head (note the use of lower case to denote contemporary stylishness and perhaps a dash of post-modern irony); but for an old-fashioned unmucked-about village local, try the Boot.

Old-fashioned, in this case, doesn't mean olde-worlde. There are no age-blackened oak beams, real or otherwise; no rows of gleaming horse-brasses or reams of hunting prints; no high-backed settles nor any other of the cliches of "traditional" pub

AT A GLANCE
Opening times:
11-2.30, 5-11
Mon-Fri; 11-11
Sat; 11-2.30-7-
11 Sun. Food
service: whenever
it's not too busy.
Big garden with
barbecues in
summer. Heated
patio with canopy.
Car park. Children
and dogs wel-
come.

décor, just a single carpeted bar (with a sort of snug ironically called "the posh end"). It's an unpretentious, functional, yet comfortable boozer so free of frills it's almost retro – like stepping back into the 1950s or early '60s, when proper locals were like people's living-rooms but with beer. (And not really with food: they'll rustle you up scampi and chips or ham egg and chips for a fiver here if you ask nicely, but this is really a pub for a beer and a gossip rather than a meal).

The beer in this case is Adnams Bitter and Broadside plus a changing guest: Greene King, the pub's former owner, wouldn't be too popular here in Dullingham. A huge rent increase back in 2000 drove a loyal tenant out, upon which the brewery promptly closed the pub and applied for plan-ning permission to turn it into a house. A local action group was formed and, under pressure, Greene King withdrew its application; in 2001 a local buyer was found and the pub was saved. But the memory lingers on...

Anyway, under independent ownership the pub has flourished. It now supports a football team, a cricket team, two crib teams and three darts teams and was Cambridge & District CAMRA's Pub of the Year in 2005.

Duxford

John Barleycorn
3 Moorfield Rd CB22 4PP

Tel 01223 832699

Surely the pub for which the word "quaint" was invented, the John Barleycorn is a long, low thatched building – possibly once a pair of cottages? – on whose frontage the not-at-all-unlikely date 1660

is proudly emblazoned. It first entered the record books as a pub, however,

AT A GLANCE
Opening times:
11-11 all week.
Food service:
12-3, 6-9.30.
Mains £7.95-
£11.95. Wifi/
internet access.
Letting rooms
£70 single, £80
double. Large car
park. Pleasant
patio. Garden
under develop-
ment. **Wheelchair
access/disabled
toilet.** Children
and dogs wel-
come.

in the early 1850s when it was called the Coach & Horses, changing its name to the John Barleycorn in the 1860s.

But don't expect to find nicotine-coloured walls, time-blackened beams and benches, little snugs and parlours, and all the other cliches of the traditional village inn here. For it has only just reopened after a complete transformation, and instead of a grizzled veteran of a boozer you will find a light, airy, spacious, uncluttered, and thoroughly modern bar-brasserie. Granted, it still embodies plenty of features from the past such as the big open fireplace and obligatory low oak-beamed ceiling complete with hop swags. But the floors are newly-laid quarry tiles; the tables are scrubbed pine; and the benches and settles are a pleasing and restful pale green.

Although the accent is on food (and there is no TV), other users are well-catered for: real ales come from Greene King, there are darts and dominoes, and the bar is usually being propped up by an assortment of non-dining locals: in fact the new landlord, Bernard Lee, was one of them himself until the opportunity to take the lease came up.

Fen Ditton

Ancient Shepherds
Green End CB5 8ST
Tel 01223 293280

The unusual name recalls a friendly society, the Loyal Order of Ancient Shepherds, which was founded in the North-West of England in 1826 and had a number of branches in the villages of East Cambridgeshire – and is in fact still going strong today with over 20,000 members.

Actually, though, there was already a pub on the site before the Loyal Order was founded. The building was originally a row of three little cottages with dormer windows like raised eyebrows, all thought to have been built in about 1540. One of them, forming today's lounge and dining room, was already licensed by 1805. The middle cottage was incorporated into the pub at some point in the 19th century and forms today's tiny public bar, which only has room for four barstools and a single bench. The third cottage, though, didn't become part of the pub until 1954 when there was a sort of reverse takeover: the owners of the cottage actually bought the pub and knocked it all through.

The result of this continuous development is a big but cosy pub, olde-worlde with low ceilings and black beams, yet very smart with an extremely comfortable lounge area with leather sofas and a giant inglenook fireplace and a very distinguished dining room. Beers are Adnams Bitter, Greene King IPA, Morland Old Speckled Hen, and a changing guest.

Fulbourn

Six Bells
9 High St CB21 5DH
Tel 01223 880244

This cheery, welcoming, and thoroughly unpretentious thatched former posting house has got things the wrong way round. In most surviving two-bar pubs it's the public bar that's cosily frowsty and dimly-lit, while the more middle-class enclosure is light and airy and uncluttered. Here they do things differently: the public bar is the light and airy and uncluttered side and could almost be somebody's verandah, while

AT A GLANCE
Opening times:
11.30-2, 6-12
Mon-Thurs;
12-12 Fri-Sat;
12-11 Sun. Food
service: 11.30-
2.30, 6-9 Mon-
Thurs; 11.30-2,
6-9.30 Fri-Sun.
Mains £6-£9.
Patio with pergola
and parasols.
Garden. Children
welcome; dogs
allowed in bar.

the larger lounge
is the bit with all
the odd nooks
and crannies,
low ceilings, and
blackened oak
beams.

Still, no-one
complains about
this breach of
decorative eti-
quette. Especially
not since the beer
(Adnams Bitter and
Broadside, Greene King IPA, Woodforde's Wherry, two guest ales and, glory of glories, a true cloudy scrumpy cider in the form of Weston's Old Rosie) is so good. Perhaps that's why it's Cambridge & District CAMRA's 2008 Pub of the Year.

Grantchester

Blue Ball
57 Broadway CB3 9NQ
Tel 01223 840697

Grantchester is one of Cambridgeshire's tourist honeypots. Visitors from far and wide make the mile-long trek across the fields from the city on foot or on bicycle, snatches of Rupert Brooke's doggerel ringing in their ears, expecting some sort of Edwardian England theme park. What they get is a tiny village, reasonably but not ravenously attractive, with four pubs (one of which is, at time of writing, closed and looking rather sorry for itself) and not very much else.

Of those four (or perhaps three) pubs there's one that not many tourists even know is there, since it's all of five minutes' walk from the village centre. Which is just as well, because the little Blue Ball in its terrace of mid-Victorian cottages (although the pub itself predates its neighbours by at least a century) couldn't really take the strain. The bigger of its two bars isn't exactly huge (there's just room for a game of ring the bull, provided you don't play it too vigorously), and the smaller snug has space for only two scrubbed pine tables. It is, however, a peach of a pub, a true boozer with no food, no telly, the oddest assortment of furniture, doubtless scrounged and haggled for over the years, and absolutely no lager. (The beer is Adnams Bitter plus a guest, and is always in lovely nick).

There's also a piano, and it's not just for show: Thursday night is music night at the Blue Ball, and the old joanna can rely on a weekly pounding from folkies, bluesmen, and exponents of any other genre of roots music who happen to be passing. The regulars are an interesting bunch, too. Few of them come from Grantchester itself: its 600 denizens are a bit upmarket for this kind of place. Instead, they tend to be liberal intellectuals – dons and researchers and the like – who walk or cycle from Cambridge and bring with them (or so the landlady says) challenging conversation and stimulating company.

Red Lion
33 High St CB3 9NF
Tel 01223 840121

 The Red Lion is quite a rare beast in England. Well, a red lion would be a rare beast anywhere; but in this case the rarity is that the Red Lion is a wholly1930s pub; and not of the mock-Tudor roadhouse variety that sprang up along the spreading network of trunk routes at that time, either, but a high-end destination pub – the sort place a well-off Cambridge chap might motor out to on a Saturday or Sunday, perhaps with his gel, for a beer and a game of bowls or perhaps just for a spot of tea in the garden.

Looking at old photos hanging in the bar, you can see that in the late 1920s there stood on this spot a tiny little Victorian pub, not much bigger than a cottage, really, with what used to be known as "pleasure gardens" (ie, a tea-shop and bowling green) attached. By the early '30s the original Red Lion, together with the house next door, had disappeared altogether, to be replaced by the building you see today. (Whose rather incongruous thatch, apparently, has come and gone over the years: in some photographs, the Red Lion is conventionally tiled; in others, thatched).

If the pub's exterior design, with its strawberry-pink paint job and its surprised-looking raised-eyebrow windows, is as neat a piece of '30s "vernacular" architecture as you'll see, then in its rambling and cavernous interior you'll find surviving examples of some of the best in pub fittings of the period. For alongside the mock-Tudor beams and absurdly fake studwork there is much well-made and attractive panelling, creating an elegant ambience that would have appealed to the well-heeled pleasure seeker of the day.

The Red Lion, as you'll have guessed, is more of a diner's than a drinker's pub, with a capacious and elegant dining-room as well as a single, but labyrinthine, bar where most of the tables seem to be laid up for food service. There's also a big garden with children's play equipment and tables and chairs shaded by parasols. But the drinker is well enough catered for with the Greene King range of cask beers including its seasonal specials.

Great Abington

Three Tuns
75 High St CB21 6AB
Tel 01223 891467
www.threetunsgreatab-
ington.co.uk

Surely everyone's dream
of the perfect English village pub, the 450-year-old
Three Tuns looks the part
both inside and out. The
main bar with its low ceilings, bare floorboards and
wood-burning stove is the
very essence of pub tradition, as is a cask beer range that
includes Greene King IPA, Adnams
Bitter, Timothy Taylor Landlord and
two guest ales. The pub is even
opposite the village cricket ground,
so you can watch the match from a
picnic table
with a cool
pint in your
hand.
It's not all
olde-worlde,
though.
An elegant
second bar
is cool and

AT A GLANCE
Opening hours:
12-2, 6-12
Mon-Fri; 11-11
Sat-Sun. Food
service: 12-2,
6-9.30 (not Sat
lunchtime). Mains
£6.50-£12. Patio
and garden. Chil-
dren and dogs
welcome.

stylish, and the Thai food for which the pub has become famous is hardly
traditional pub fare. There's also wifi and internet access for those who
just can't leave their laptops at home.
A five-bedroom accommodation block was due to open in April, with
rooms at £70 a night. The block also contains disabled toilets.

Hardwick

Blue Lion
Main St CB3 7QU Tel 01954 210328

A pub so cute you could eat it, the Blue Lion with its low tiled roof and dormers is about as
quaint as they come – and is bright yellow, not blue. Actually, the rather unusual name is a
good clue as to the pub's age: the blue lion was part of the coat of arms of Anne of Den-
mark, wife of James I, which places it in the first 20 years of the 17th century.

Inside there are, as you would expect, low ceilings, black beams, stone floors, real ales (from Greene King) and an open fire. The two bars have, as is now almost universal, been knocked into one; although the fact that they're on different levels, and that the studwork of the partition that once divided them remains in place, gives them very different characters. (The split levels throughout the pub may create atmosphere but make disabled access, alas, a practical impossibility).

AT A GLANCE
Opening times: 12-11 all week. Food service: 12-3, 6-9 all week. Mains £6-£12.99. Carvery on Sunday. Children yes. Dogs no.

With its stripped pine tables, leather-covered seating, woodburning stove and lack of clutter, the Blue Lion is no temple to antiquity but is a smart, comfortable, and welcoming reinterpretation of the traditional pub. There's also a cosy dining room with conservatory, a big garden with play equipment, and an attractive seating area at the front.

Harlton

Hare & Hounds
High St CB23 1ES
Tel 01223 262672
www.thehareandhoundspub.net

An oddly-proportioned building, the tall, thin Hare & Hounds has the look of an ancient cottage to which an improbably thatched upper story was added in Victorian times. The impression is strengthened by the abundance of oak beams inside, which are clearly structural rather than decorative, and by the fact that it wasn't recorded as a pub until 1879.

At that time it was one of four pubs in Harlton; but all the others have long since fallen by the wayside, leaving the Hare & Hounds to lubricate and entertain the village on its own. This is a job it does superbly well, subscribing wholeheartedly to the apt philosophy that a good local has something for everyone. For the beer drinker there are Eagle and Bombardier from Charles Wells, plus a guest; for the

AT A GLANCE

Opening times:
12-3, 5-11 Tues-
Fri; 12-11 Sat;
12-5, 7-10.30
Sun; 5-11 Mon.
Food service:
12-2, 6-9 Tues-
Fri; 12-2.30
Sat-Sun. Mains
£5-£11.95;
baguettes £3.95.
Heated patio.
Large garden.
Children and
dogs welcome.

hungry there's a wide-ranging and well-priced menu, as well as barbecues in the garden in summer and popular themed evenings offering tapas, Tex-Mex, curries and other exotica on Saturdays; for those in need of entertainment there's darts, crib and petanque (the pub also supports a cricket team); for the smoker there's a heated and sheltered patio; for the simply cold there's a big inglenook fireplace.

Hinxton

Red Lion
32 High St CB10 1QY
Tel 01799 530601

The Red Lion must have one of the largest pub car parks in Cambridgeshire – and it needs it! A rambling 16th-century building with jettied front, all painted in striking Tudor pink, it sums up what many people must dream of when they say the words "village inn".

AT A GLANCE

Opening hours:
11-3, 6-11 Mon-
Sat, 12-4, 7-10.30
Sun. Food service: 12-2, 6.45-9
Mon-Thurs;
12-2.30, 7-9.30
Fri-Sat; 7-9 Sun.
Soups and starters £4.50-£5;
mains £6-£11.
Garden and
patio. Children
welcome. **Wheelchair access /
disabled toilet.**

The big L-shaped bar with its cosy nooks and crannies, its pretty Victorian cast-iron fire surround, its apparently random assortment of sofas and settles, its clutter of clocks and ornaments, doesn't disappoint the dreamer either. But the modern world is not forgotten: there are ramps and loos for wheelchair users, and wifi and internet for those umbilically joined to the internet. The separate restaurant at the back is also a modern addition, although you wouldn't guess to look at it; and eight letting rooms (£80 single, £95 double) have just opened in a separate building.

Histon

Red Lion
68 High St CB24 9JD
Tel 01223 564437

A bustling village that's more of a small town really, Histon has plenty of attractive and welcoming pubs. What marks the Red Lion at the top of the High Street out from the rest is its commitment to beer. Not just real ales, either. There are never fewer than seven of them – Theakston Bitter, Oakham Bishop's Farewell, Everard's Tiger, Tring Blonde and Mighty Oak Oscar Wilde Mild are the regulars – and there's a fridgeful of strong Belgian bottled beers as well. And a traditional perry.

AT A GLANCE
Opening times: 10.30-3, 4-11 Mon-Thurs; 10.30-3, 4-12 Fri; 10.30-11 Sat; 12-11 Sun. Food service: 12-2 Mon-Sat. Mains £5-£8. Small car park. Nice garden.

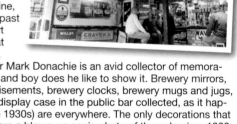

But there's more than that. The place is a shrine, a temple, to breweries past and present – and apart from the pumpclips that cover the entire ceiling, mostly past. Pub owner Mark Donachie is an avid collector of memorabilia of past breweries, and boy does he like to show it. Brewery mirrors, brewery enamel advertisements, brewery clocks, brewery mugs and jugs, brewery ashtrays (in a display case in the public bar collected, as it happens, by my Dad in the 1930s) are everywhere. The only decorations that aren't brewery-related are a blown-up sepia photo of the pub, circa 1900, advertising tea (!), and a surely ironic smattering of horse-brasses and the like on the chimney of the lounge bar fireplace. Oh, and there are regular beer festivals too.

Linton

Crown
11 High St CB1 6HS Tel 01223 891759 www.crownatlinton.co.uk

A very affluent South Cambridgeshire village, all narrow streets lined with picturesque houses, Linton could well be used a location for a BBC costume drama, and in the Crown it has the inn it deserves.

An 18th-century posting house by origin, its interior retains all the period charm you could ask for. What was once a warren of low-ceilinged, heavily-beamed little bars has been knocked into one long, narrow space, but it's all on different levels and there are plenty of nooks and corners

AT A GLANCE
Opening times:
12-3, 5.30-11
Mon-Sat; 12-8
Sun. Food service
12-2, 7-9.30 Mon-
Sat; 12-3 Sun.
Sandwiches from
£4.50 (lunchtime
only); mains £10-
£17.50. Patio.
Car park through
archway. Wifi/
internet access.
Children and
dogs welcome.

to be private in. The grand fireplace at the front is a cheerful survival of past glories.

Very much a well-heeled dining pub, it also has a respectable selection of cask ales in Greene King IPA, Woodforde's Wherry, and a changing guest. Lots of steps, but a double door gives wheelchair access to the dining room. The five letting rooms are £59.95 a night including breakfast.

Little Wilbraham

Hole in the Wall
2 High St CB21 5JY
Tel 01223 812282
www.the-holeinthewall.com

There's no shortage of great places to eat in the affluent country villages that surround Cambridge, and the Hole in the Wall is one of the finest of them.

Thought to date from the 15th century, it comes complete with close-set upright studwork, oak beams garlanded with swags of dried hops, and a big bare-brick open fireplace. The Hole in the Wall itself was was supposedly a serving hatch through which jugs of ale were passed out to parched farmworkers; the spot where it it is said to have been is marked by a plaque and inscription. (The ale that would be passed out were the hatch still open being Woodforde's Wherry and a choice of two guests). The dining room is a much more modern extension, but blends harmoniously with the ancient main building.

But it's not so much the history and the beer that draw people from far and wide

as the food. Chef-patron Christopher Leeton has a grand track record on the other side of the country, where he cooked in Shropshire for Shaun Hill of Merchant's House, Ludlow, fame and then for Stephen Bull at the Loughpool Inn in Herefordshire. He and wife Jenny set up on their own here in 2005 and immediately started winning awards with menus featuring produce almost entirely sourced from the neighbourhood (except the fish, of course!). A reasonably-priced lunchtime menu starts at £3.50 for soup of the day and goes up to fish pie at £12.50, while the evening menu ranges from starters such as smoked Bressingham duck at £5.50 through to mains such as braised fillet of halibut at £17.50. East Anglian cheeses are a speciality.

Madingley

Three Horseshoes
High St CB3 8AB
Tel 01954 210221
www.threehorseshoesmadingley.
co.uk

One of Cambridgeshire's premier dining pubs, the Three Horseshoes was until recently one of the Huntsbridge Group of gastropubs but is now back in independent ownership. It's still not a place for the faint-hearted, though: its cheapest starter is a bowl of olives at £3, while a pot-roasted fillet of beef wrapped in coppa di parma with roasted trevise and soft polenta with butter, parmesan, and gremolata will set you back £23 (veg extra). That's if you eat in the restaurant, mind: in the bar, a starter of grilled pig's trotter with lentils would be £6, with lasagne and salad at £10. Expensive, yes; but it is, however, worth it.

And neither the Three Horseshoes' foodie fame, nor the restaurant prices, nor the cool, contemporary, chic décor of pale paintwork and polished floorboards put off the villagers, who still pop in for a pint (Adnams Bitter, a guest ale, and Dunkerton's Organic Cider from Herefordshire) as they have been doing since at least 1765 when the pub was first recorded.

Which date makes the thatched Three Horseshoes one of the oldest buildings in the village, which belonged in its entirety to the Hinde Cotton family from the middle ages until 1871. They built the magnificent Madingley Hall in 1542 (much altered in 1910 and now the property of Cambridge University) but otherwise permitted very little building on their estate. They did put up some new houses in 1821 and 1841; but there are few buildings of earlier date in Madingley, and the Three Horseshoes is one of 'em. (Incidentally, the Hall was rented out to Queen Victoria in the 1860s as digs for the Prince of Wales, later Edward VII, while he was studying, or pretending to study, at Cambridge. Did he ever slip out for a sly one at the Shoes? With his reputation, quite probably.)

Milton

Waggon & Horses
39 High St CB24 6DF
Tel 01223 860313

In a village that has three much prettier and far more ancient pubs, the Waggon & Horses is not the obvious standout. But it's not the Jolly Brewers (closed at time of writing), nor the Lion & Lamb, nor the White Horse that attract all the attention, whatever their undoubted merits. It's the apparently workaday Waggon & Horses with its brewer's Tudor fake beams (dating from circa 1934, when it replaced a much, much older pub on the site) that has consistently been endorsed by beer-lovers as Milton's best.

This goes back to the 1990s and beyond, when the Waggon & Horses was a free house that served ale from cult brewers such as Bateman's and Nethergate while its rivals were tied to national brands. Then in 1999 the Waggon & Horses itself became a tied house when it was bought by Elgood's of Wisbech – the first pub the brewery had bought for 55 years, actually, and its most southerly outpost. Would the tie make the Waggon & Horses boring?

No. The Elgood's range (always including a dark mild) plus a guest beer plus farmhouse cider from Cassel's of Great Shelford was exciting enough to retain the devotion of local Campaign for Real Ale members, and the Waggon & Horses, despite its single big bar and swirly pub carpets, keeps winning awards and endorsements from those who know their beer.

It helps that the tenant, Nick Winnington, is something of a legend in beer circles, having been in the trade for over 40 years and a CAMRA member for over 30. His previous billet was the equally legendary Cambridge Blue, and the enormous collection of hats are all his – they date back to the early 1970s, when he thought it might be amusing to wear a bowler on duty. It was. Someone brought him another hat to try on, and someone else brought another, and so it went on. Bring him a new one, and if it's sufficiently eccentric he'll stand you a pint.

AT A GLANCE
Opening times: 12-2.30, 5-11 Mon-Thurs-Fri; 12-3, 6-11.30 Sat; 12-3, 7-10.30 Sun. Food service: 12-2, 7-9. Snacks from £1.50. Mains £5-£6. Limited parking. Covered smoking shelter. Big garden with play equipment. Children to 9pm. Dogs welcome.

Newton

Queens Head
Fowlmere Rd CB22 7PG Tel 01223 870436

A puzzle pub, this. The moment you walk in you know you've found the perfect pub, but when you try to describe it to a third party, you can't put your finger on what's so special about it. Let me demonstrate.

The Queen's Head is a small brick building of the late 17th century, standing on foundations that are perhaps 200 years older, and with an extension dating from 1835. In the older part is a comfortable saloon bar with low ceilings, an ancient quarry-tile floor, and a big fireplace. The newer part is the public bar. It too has quarry-tiled floors and a big fireplace, and is fitted out with a long refectory table, bum-numbingly narrow benches, and a rickety-looking round-backed settle. The walls are adorned with original watercolours and pencil drawings and, rather incongruously, a stuffed goose and a stuffed duck in glass cases.

The beer is from Adnams: Bitter, Broadside, and the seasonal. Traditional cider is from Crone's of Norfolk, with Cassel's in bottle. Food is soup (sold by colour), fresh-cut sandwiches, or baked potatoes, all at under a fiver. Games are crib, darts, shove ha'penny, and table skittles. No garden, but there are picnic tables in the small car park and on a patch of green across the road.

AT A GLANCE
Opening times: 11.30-2.30, 6-11 Mon-Sat. 12-2.30, 7-10.30 Sun. Food service 12-2, 7-9.30 Mon-Sat; 12-2, 7-9 Sun. Children allowed in games room. Dogs welcome.

Doesn't sound much, does it? But everything is somehow right. The beer is always as good as beer can be; and you should see the joints of beef and ham that landlord David Short carves for your sandwiches! But what is it that transforms these good but everyday things into something magical? As a writer, I shouldn't really admit that words sometimes fail me. But sometimes, they do.

Reach

Dyke's End
8 Fair Green CB25 0JD
Tel 01638 743816

**The people of Reach have fought hard for their pub; and if they have a slightly self-satisfied air as they enjoy their dinners there, well, they've done more than most pubgoers to earn it.
The last pub in the tiny village, the White Horse, was closed by Watney's in 1967. Eight years later a thirsty villager**

put the giant brewery's error right by converting his own house, overlooking the long green that gives the village its name ("recce" is Old English for a stretch or strip), into a pub which he called the King's. But perhaps the bean-counters at Watney's hadn't erred quite so much in their judgement after all, for Reach is not much more than a hamlet, with not enough potential customers to guarantee a living; and in the next 15 years the King's, despite winning plaudits both for its beer and its food, hit financial bad patches more than once.

Finally in 1998 landlord Bill Lester, having failed to sell the King's as a going concern, applied for planning permission to change it back into a house. But determined not to lose their pub, a group of villagers got together to rescue it. In a campaign that lasted nearly two years they first blocked the planning application and then raised enough money to buy and refurbish the King's, which reopened under its new name, the Dyke's End (the Devil's Dyke is a Saxon earthwork that runs for seven miles from Woodditton to Reach), in October 1999 with chef Phil Vincent as lessee.

AT A GLANCE
Opening times: 12-2.30, 6-11 Mon-Sat. 12-11 Sun. Food service: 12-1.45, 6-8.45 Tues-Sat; 12-2 Sun. Mains £9.95-£15.45. Smaller portions £4.95. Small car park . Secluded garden. Patio overlooks village green. Children and dogs welcome. **Wheelchair access/disabled toilet**.

In 2003 – the same year that Prince Charles, as patron of the Pub is the Hub campaign, dropped in for a congratulatory pint – a new lessee, barrister and part-time judge Frank Feehan, came along ; hence the prints of judges in full regalia that hang in the bar. In 2007 he and his brother Martin opened the brewery in the outbuildings behind the pub that supplies most of its beer.

Well, the villagers certainly have the pub they deserve. The ground-floor bar is both comfortable and classy, with has a farmhouse kitchen feel with beams, a big fireplace, scrubbed pine tables, and bare floorboards at one end and a more elegant Georgian-style panelled walls at the other; while elegance is also the keynote of the upstairs dining room. And if tiny Reach doesn't have quite enough people to ensure the Dyke's End's continued survival, there are enough enthusiastic visitors from further afield to do more than just keep it afloat. But if you're considering making the trip, a word of warning: the pub is set back from the street and its sign is discreet to the point of invisibility. So a clue: it's opposite the war memorial.

Shepreth

Plough
SG8 6PP
Tel 01763 260523
www.theploughshepreth.co.uk

From the outside, the Plough is an unextraordinary brick-built Victorian village pub. Only the signboard, which is kinda funky in a minimalist sort of groove, betrays any hint of the unusual. Then you go inside and it's like, wow! What the? is a sleepy Cambridgeshire village like Shepreth doing with a joint like this?

You've got the highly-polished bare floorboards alternating with the cool Mediterranean tiles. You've got the cubic leather armchairs. You've got the round black tabletops. You've got the brushed steel dining chairs. You've got the huge abstracts by a, like, local artist, you know? You've got Zaphod Beeblebrox and Ford Prefect enjoying a pan-Galactic gargleblaster in a quiet corner with Slartibartfast and the triple-breasted whore of Eroticon 3 ... well, no, you haven't, actually, but in such a context the ultramodernity of the Plough's interior is such a shock that you might as well have.

But that's enough of space-age interior design.

AT A GLANCE

Opening times: 12-3, 6-11 Tues-Sun. Food service: 12-2, 6-9 Tues-Sun. Mains £10-£18. Bar menu £9-£12. Lovely gardens. Car park. Children welcome; dogs not.

The question is: is the Plough still a pub? Well, when they say they don't have peanuts but they can bring you a bowl of olives for £2 you think, mmm, maybe not. But then the Adnams Bitter is fine, and they put on a second cask beer in summer when the gardens that surround the pub on three sides fill up with Shepreth folk who are just out for a pint, not award-winning cuisine. So although it's a damn fine judgement, yes, on balance the Plough is still a pub. And quite a nice one, actually.

Swaffham Prior

Red Lion
High St CB5 0LD
Tel 01638 745483

It's a rare thing to see in a pub, but nice all the same – oak beams that are not only functional and structural, but are also the natural colour of oak. Because oak isn't really black. Only the Victorians decided that it should be, and went around with the pitchpot coating every beam in

sight until we were all fooled into thinking that, yeah, oak is black. But it isn't. It's a lustrous dark gold – just like the beams here, in fact.

Golden-hued oak beams in quite some profusion aren't the only rarity here. The pub is also overlooked by not one but two church towers – and both St Mary's and St Cyriac's are in the same churchyard, which is unique. To pile curiosity upon curiosity, both towers are octagonal, which, again, is... well, this isn't about them. It's about the Red Lion.

Which is a lovely, snug, little 17th-century alehouse with all the low ceilings, quarry-tiled floors, and cheerful open fireplaces you'd expect of such a place. There are some horse-brasses, too,

AT A GLANCE
Opening times:
12-3, 6-11.30.
Food service:
12-2, 6-9. Mains
£7.45-£10.45.
Greene King
beers. Small car
park. Secluded
garden. Children
and dogs wel-
come.

but in moderation, and
some quaint old local
photographs, and some
historical research that tells
you that today's kitchen
was built in the 1800s as a
club-room where dances,
trade union meetings, and
even Chapel meetings were
held (until a proper Chapel
was built, that is).

And what's nice is that although food is obviously very important, it's still quite clearly a village local with plenty of time and space for barstools and the good old boys that go with them.

Thriplow

Green Man
2 Lower St
SG8 7RJ
Tel 01763 208855
www.green-
manthriplow.
co.uk

Should a pub called the Green Man, that overlooks a village green, really be painted such a very dark blue? Shouldn't it be painted green? Or is the landlord trying to make a point of some sort?

Be that as it may, the Green Man's interior is nothing like as crepuscular as its square Victorian façade, but is light and airy and, other than the pumpclips from guest ales gone by stuck all over the ceiling, relatively uncluttered. The walls are cream, the floorboards are stripped, the furniture is contemporary (including enormous square leather barstools, for those whose posteriors are too large for the regular kind).

The Green Man has made its name as a food pub in an area dominated by food pubs – scarcely a mile down the road it has formidable competition in the shape of the Chequers at Fowlmere – but they insist here that it's a pub with food rather than a restaurant with beer; and given the number of customers sitting without plates in front of them, they're right. And the beers are important here: there are up to four real ales at a time, always changing, and with no permanent bitter so you never know what you're going to get. Only that it will be good.

AT A GLANCE
Opening times:
12-3, 7-11
Tues-Sat; 12-3
Sun. (Closed
Sun evening and
all Mon). Food
service: 12-2, 7-9.
Tiny car park.
Secluded patio/
garden. Children
welcome.

Waterbeach

Bridge Hotel
Clayhithe Rd, CB5 9HZ
Tel 01223 860622

Now effectively part of Waterbeach, Clayhithe used to be a working village with busy wharf on the Cam. Not many people actually live there now – there's a scattering of farms and cottages, but not what you'd really call a village – which makes the very existence of such a big pub as the Bridge all the more extraordinary. Especially as it's comparatively modern.

By the time the pub was built in 1875, on the site of an alehouse called at various times the Pike & Eel, the Jack & Eel, and the House of Lords, Clayhithe's economic glory days as a loading point for lighters carrying local bricks up the Cam to the Ouse and, eventually, the North Sea had already all but gone. But the company that built a toll-bridge here in 1872-5, replacing a ferry known since the 14th century, decided to make a resort of it, so the newly-built Clayhithe Bridge Hotel had tea gardens and even a menagerie with its own bear. Pleasure steamers from Cambridge stopped here regularly and, of course, it was also a convenient resort for anglers.

So really you can disregard all the hop-swagged beams you'll see in the Bridge's cavernous interior (and you'll see lots!) and also the skeletal stud walls that seem to recall medieval internal partitions. But don't let them spoil your enjoyment of the pub's riotously busy bar and three dining rooms with their stone fireplaces and their little nooks and quiet crannies and their pleated, frilled, and deep-swagged curtains (great for absorbing noise) and their bits and bobs and bric-a-brac. This is a place that was built for pleasure and, sitting out on a warm evening on its delightful riverside terrace with a cool pint of ale (Courage Directors', Charles Wells Bombardier, or the guest ale) in your hand, you'll agree that the builders succeeded.

AT A GLANCE
Opening times: 11-11, 12-10.30 all week. Food service 11-10 Mon-Sat; 12-9 Sun. Light lunch £6.95 for two courses. Mains £6.40-£14.20. Sunday roasts. Big car park. **Wheelchair access/disabled toilet**. Children yes; dogs no.

Whittlesford

Bees In The Wall
36 North Rd CB22 4NZ
Tel 01223 834289

There really are bees in the wall at the Bees in the Wall – a colony of masonry beers has bored its way into a wonderfully warm spot just next to the chimney. But until the 1950s the Bees in the Wall was known as the Exhibition; so if you thought you were gazing at an early

Victorian villa, you're right, since the name dates it neatly to 1851 when the Great Exhibition was opened in Hyde Park, in the enormous greenhouse designed by the Duke of Devonshire's gardener, Joseph Paxton. (Later removed to Crystal Palace and eventually burnt down).

Sharing a village with the majestic Tickell Arms (see next entry) must rather cast a shadow over any humbler pub's food offering; but the Bees in the Wall is actually mostly dining room and its food offering isn't half bad. There's plenty of honest pub food running up to steak at £13.95 and a posher menu on Fridays and Saturdays that includes venison at £14.95. (Thursday is fish and chip night).

AT A GLANCE
Opening times: 11-2.30, 6-11 Mon-Sat; 11-2.30, 6-10.30 sun. Food service 12-2 every day; 7-9 Wed-Sat. Children welcome.

As well as its comfortable split-level dining room, though, the Bees in the Wall has a proper public bar with open fire, high-backed settles, cribbage, and darts, where Timothy Taylor Landlord is the regular ale alongside two guests.

The Bees in the Wall must also be one of the few pubs in the country, if not the only pub in the country, to boast its own woods – just nice for a bracing walk before lunch and a pint in the garden.

Tickell Arms
North Rd CB2 4NZ Tel 01223 833128 www.tickellarms.co.uk

There's a fine line between gastropub and out-and-out restaurant; and by virtue of having real ale (specially brewed by Brandon Brewery of Suffolk and served from stillage: the antique china handpumps are just for show) and of setting aside Sunday evenings for drinkers only, the Tickell just shades it as a pub.

Dogs are welcome, too, which definitely makes it a pub. But what a pub! Its classical façade painted azure blue (the ground colour of the Tickell coat of arms), embellished with quite extraordinary Regency wrought-iron windows and arched front door, and approached through a rank of stone lions and urns, tells you that this is something far grander than a mere pub. Once inside you're in a bar, true, but one stuffed with antiques. And as for the dining room – its bottle-green walls, grand fireplace, and gleaming mahogany tables belong more to a small stately home than a pub.

And yet it's been a pub for a very long time, having been first recorded as the Waggon & Horses in 1810, when it was a posting house on the London-Cambridge turnpike. After the war it was taken over by the lord of the manor, Joseph Hollick de la Taste Tickell, known to all as Kim, who bestowed his family name on it and earned himself a reputation both for eccentricity – knee-breeches and silver-buckled shoes were his costume of choice – and extraordinary rudeness.

A prominent notice banning lefties grew longer and longer over the years and eventually extended the ban to categories of society that may not legally be banned today. And as often happens when extraordinary rudeness is guaran-teed, the Tickell Arms rapidly became famous and people would queue up to be insulted, paying hand-somely for the pleasure.

Tickell died in 1990, and since late 2007 the chef-patron has been Michael Henry Burgoyne, a Nico Ladenis-trained chef and a quarter Breton, who has brought with him a passion for local produce (including, the mark of a true Breton, local farmhouse cider) and French regional cookery. But while his cooking undoubt-edly constitutes fine dining, he has striven to ensure that you can eat here without having to sell the Porsche. Soup in the bar is just £4.50, while a club sandwich on bread baked in the kitchen (he churns his own butter, too) is only £7. On the other hand, you could treat yourself to three courses including seared red mullet, roast fillet of beef marinière de Valence and galette bretonne with Grand Marnier blackberries in the magnificent dining room for £35.95.

AT A GLANCE

Opening times: 12-2.30, 7-11 Tues-Sun. Food served 12-2.30, 7-9.30 Tues-Sat, 12-2.30 Sun. Family Sunday lunch £17.95 for three courses. Formal garden with ornamental pond and wild-fowl. Wifi/internet access.

Woodditton

Three Blackbirds
36 Ditton Green CB8 9SQ.
Tel 01638 730811.
www.threeblackbirds.com

The charming, thatched Three Blackbirds bears its birthdate,1642, proudly over its front door – a date that makes it one of the oldest surviving houses in the collection of scattered hamlets that makes up Woodditton.

In a way it's odd that so little survives of the village's historic buildings, since it sits at one end of one of the region's most historic monuments. The Devil's Dyke is a seven-mile long earthwork that originally stood 50ft tall from ditch bottom to bank top and formed the boundary between the

Saxon kingdoms of East Anglia and Mercia. You can still walk the whole length of the Dyke, which has been expensively conserved; and if you work up a suitable thirst en route there's another pub at the far end, the aptly-named Dyke's End at Reach.

Despite its 17th-century roots, the Three Blackbirds wasn't recorded as a pub until it was listed as the Blackbird Inn in a trade directory of 1764. Until comparatively recently it was one of many in Woodditton – another trade directory lists three "beer retailers" in 1900 in Ditton Green alone, although only the Blackbirds is named as a pub – and during World War II it and the Marquis of Granby shared the custom of the local Home Guard. Their Sunday morning parades were held outside each in turn, and the order "dismiss" mysteriously coincided with opening time. The Marquis, though, closed in 1955 and has since been demolished, leaving the Three Blackbirds as the last survivor.

It's as charming inside as it is out, with brick fireplaces in both the bar and the small, cosy front dining-room, quarry-tiled floors, beams aplenty, and old photos of local interest. There's also a bigger, smarter dining-room in the flint-built rear extension and yet a third – a small one ideal for intimate private parties – upstairs.

AT A GLANCE

Opening times (subject to change when new licensee takes over): 12-2, 7-9.30 Mon-Sat; 12-2 Sun. Food service as above. Cask beers from Greene King range. Big car park and garden. Children welcome; dogs welcome in the bar.

Brandon Creek

Ship
Brandon Creek Bridge PE38 0PP
Tel 01353 676228

Strategically sited where the Little and Great Ouses meet, and where the Little Ouse is crossed by the King's Lynn-Ely road, the Ship has long been a welcome sight to weary wayfarers both waterborne and on foot. And not just because a pub is always a welcome sight at the end of a hard day, but because this corner of the fens is, statistically speaking, the most desolate part of South-Eastern England. It has the broadest stretches of countryside without public roads and human habitations within a 100-mile radius of London, so the sight of a pub would not only be most welcome but also something of a surprise.

How long the Ship has been surprising and delighting footsore wayfarers is anybody's guess. The present building is quite clearly Victorian; but legend has it being used as a lock-up during the Civil War, when some Royalist prisoners escaped by murdering the landlord and landlady but were recaptured and hanged on the riverbank. Legend also has it that Mark Twain once stayed here; and that there are three ghosts, a man, a woman, and a child.

Well, pubs always attract legends, especially pubs in lonely places like

AT A GLANCE
Opening times: 12-2.30, 7-11 Tues-Sun. Food served 12-2.30, 7-9.30 Tues-Sat, 12-2.30 Sun. Family Sunday lunch £17.95 for three courses. Formal garden with ornamental pond and wildfowl. Wifi/internet access.

this (or at least it would be lonely, if it weren't for the A10). But one cast-iron historical truth that the Ship can demonstrate as fact is the long link between blacksmiths' forges and alehouses, for it shared its site with a forge for very many years. Three generations of the Turner family ran the smithy until horse-drawn barges finally disappeared in the 1950s, for barge horses needed shoeing just as much as dray horses, carriage horses, and riding horses; and while the Turners shod them, the Ship used to stable them for a shilling a night. The derelict forge was finally demolished in 1982 to make way for the single-storey extension you see today, which was part of a complete internal rebuild that took eight months. The refurbished pub was officially declared open by Jack Turner, the last of the family to have worked in the forge.

There's nothing desolate about the Ship today. Comfortable and cheery in a homely sort of way, it comprises a single big split-level bar with deep carpets and soft furnishings with a 40-seater restaurant overlooking the broad open water where the two rivers meet. The terrace also overlooks the river and is understandably crowded on sunny days. Adnams Bitter is the regular cask beer, and there are two guest ales in winter and three in summer.

Castor

Prince of Wales Feathers
38 Peterborough Rd PE5 7AL
Tel 01733 380222
www.princeofwalesfeathers.co.uk

The bustling hub of a bustling village, the handsome double-fronted Victorian Prince of Wales Feathers works its socks off to keep the people of Castor entertained whether their tastes run to pastimes ancient or modern. Alongside the sports on satellite TV, the Sunday night quizzes, the Saturday night live bands, and the pool table with regular tournaments, there are more traditional games available – and not just darts and crib, either, but rarities like shove ha'penny and shut the box.

And although it's strictly speaking a one-bar pub, there are plenty of odd corners where you can get away from all this frantic activity and enjoy your beer (Woodforde's Wherry, Adnams Bitter, John Smith's, and two guests) in peace. The darts and table games have a room to themselves, as does the pool, and the bar itself is subdivided to provide a lounge area with a battered but comfy leather three-piece suite beside the fire.

Chatteris

Cross Keys
Market Hill PE16 6BA
Tel 01354 693036
www.crosskeyshotel-chatteris
.com

Chatteris, it has to be admitted, is not the most charming of towns, but in the Cross Keys it has a hotel of unique character whose plain white-painted rendered frontage conceals an architectural jigsaw that would keep a connoisseur of ancient buildings happy for weeks.

The Victoria County History puts the inn's age at around 300 years (and records, by the way, that in the 1930s it had a thatched roof that must have seemed somewhat incongruous); but more recent excavations indicate that the Georgian front hides an inn going back to around 1540, when it was built using architectural salvage quarried from the town's nunnery, closed during the Dissolution of the Monasteries in the 1530s. But it may well be that even that early phase was only a rebuilding of a medieval hospice connected with the church of St Peter & St Paul opposite, the crossed keys being a symbol of St Peter's;

AT A GLANCE

Opening times:
11.30-2.30; 6.30-
11. Food service:
12-2, 7-6 Sun-
Thurs; 12-2, 7-9.30
Fri-Sat. Sandwich-
es, light lunches
£3.50-£6.95; mains
£8.95-£15.45. Real
ales: Greene King
range. 12 letting
rooms: £30-£52
single; £40-£78
double. Car park.
Patio. Children
allowed in dining
rooms until 10pm;
dogs allowed in
bar.

and etched into the back of an ancient millstone preserved in the yard are not only a set of crossed keys but also what appears to be a crescent moon – a link with the Crusades, perhaps?

Then six years ago the hotel was extended into the row of derelict cottages next door, and during the conversion work the apparent remains of a cross-passage and solar were discovered; so even these humble cottages appear to have had a much more significant past as a medieval hall-house of quite high status.

The result of all the many phases of development is a delightful warren of a place, much bigger than its modest street frontage would suggest. The conversion of the cottages and the roofing over of the courtyard have created no fewer than five dining rooms, ranging from intimate to spacious, each with its own character and charm. The lounge bar, which occupies the oldest part of the original inn, is elegantly kitted out with black leather sofas and armchairs and subtly lit by table lamps and has two big fireplaces adorned with a medley of implements including a brass mulling funnel originally intended to be filled with beer and thrust right into the fire.

Walk the Dog

34 Bridge St
PE16 6RN
Tel 01354 693695

A greater contrast with the Cross Keys could scarcely be imagined. A straightforward mid-Victorian roadhouse, probably dating from the period 1830-69 when the Beer Act allowed householders to sell beer and cider without a

AT A GLANCE

Opening times:
11-2.30, 5-11
Mon-Thurs; 11-11
Fri-Sat; 11-4.30,
7-10.30 Sun.
Food service:
12-2 Fri-Sat; 12-3
Sun. Sandwiches,
hot snacks up to
£5. Roast on Sun-
days. Car park
across Pound
Lane. Covered
patio. Children
and dogs wel-
come.

licence, the Walk The Dog is an uncomplicated and indeed near-perfect example of the kind of community local that our Government is giving such a hard time these days.

Its white-painted, south-facing, open-plan bar fills with sunshine on pleasant days but has a cheerful open fire for when the days aren't so pleasant. It's a proper beer-drinker's pub: you can get sandwiches and hot meals for up to a fiver, but only on Fridays, Saturdays, and Sundays, and the real ales – Charles Wells Bombardier and up to five guests – are definitely the main attraction. And the covered smoking area has to be among the best-equipped in Cambridgeshire, with leather-covered bar settles and a proper fireplace.

But it's the pub's name that sets it apart. They're used to unusual names in these parts: up the road in one direction is Nightlayer's Fen; in the other is Womb Farm. The pub was originally called the Ship, then the New Ship; about a dozen years ago it adopted its new name as a sort of double-edged joke. Men, of course, have always used walking the dog as an excuse for a swift half or two; but the real joke was that at the time of the name change dogs weren't allowed in. They are now.

Black Horse

PE8 6RU
Tel 01832 280240

The neo-classical Black Horse with its handsome stone façade was built by the Elton Hall estate in the late 17th century, and shows that even at this early date the coaching and posting trades were already of sufficient economic significance to make such a considerable investment worth the risk. It fronts the feeder from Oundle that met the Great North Road at Alwalton; and as building it cannot have been cheap it's fair to suppose that its early patrons must have been pretty well-heeled and therefore demanding.

Its ambience today is still affluent. Its interior is traditional, with a fair few beams and an enormous fireplace; but the good furniture and parquet floors speak more of the Georgian than the olde-worlde. The main dining room is particularly smart, and there are a couple of intimate little side-rooms for more private dining as well; and there's an à la carte menu with mains from £10.95-£14.95 (vegetables from the pub's own garden) to match.

AT A GLANCE
Opening times: 12-11 Mon-Thurs; 12-12 Fri-Sat; 12-7 Sun. Food service: 12-2, 6.30-9 Mon-Thurs; 12-2.30 6.30-9.30 Fri-Sat; 12-3 Sun. Set menu £11.50 for two courses, £14.50 for three. Lighter lunches £5.75-£8.95. Real ales: Everards Tiger, Oakham JHB, one from Digfield range; one guest. Wifi/internet access. Car park across the road. Children and dogs welcome.

Let's not get too carried away with all this opulence, though: a room at the back was once Elton's lock-up, and the landlord in the 1940s and '50s was Harry Kirk, the hangman who officiated at Nuremburg and did the honours for both James Hanratty and Ruth Ellis.

A striking feature of the Black Horse is its enormous garden. The old terrace is big enough; but landlord John Clennel has begged the top end of the adjoining paddock from the Elton Hall estate as well, and in summer he puts up goalposts, a badminton net, and even a volleyball net. He'll take them all down on Sunday afternoons this summer, though, for a series of open-air jazz concerts for which he's booked some pretty well-known performers.

Cutter
Annesdale, Station Rd
CB7 4BN
Tel 01353 662713

With its long river front-age and its bright, sunny principal rooms, the Cutter is understandably one of the most popular pubs in Ely. Which makes it all the more annoying that it's also one of the hardest to find! The street it's in is too tiny to appear on anything but the largest-scale city map; but don't despair. Leave the city centre and cathedral behind you and head down Back Hill. Straight over the roundabout and just before you reach the station there's a little left turn called Annesdale, at the end of which is the Cutter. Don't be put off, either, by the minute car park that is apparently considered sufficient for such a well-used Ely institution: there's another one, and much bigger, at the back.

Converted from a pair of cottages in 1830 to serve workers on the new wharf that had just been completed, the Cutter was part of an enormous industrial complex that also included a maltings, a 13-barrel brewery, a house, offices, stabling for 14 horses, and a separate bar called the Cutter Tap. It wasn't an immediate success. It changed hands six times between 1837 and 1847; it was unoccupied for several short periods, during one of which the brewery copper was stolen; and several landlords were prosecuted for offences ranging from late opening to keeping a disorderly house. But as industry gave way to leisure, the riverside quarter became more tranquil; and the Cutter became more genteel with it. The old dock became a marina, and anglers and weekend sailors replaced dockers, prostitutes and boatmen as the pub's customers.

AT A GLANCE
Opening times: 11-11.30 Mon-Sun. Food service: 12-9 Mon-Sun. Mains £8-£17; Sunday roast £9.95. Riverside terrace. Children welcome.

A major refurbishment in 2006 transformed the Cutter's interior into a bright, airy and thoroughly modern space, with a big main bar that is uncluttered to the point of minimalist and whose counter is actually half a boat (there are blown-up pictures of it being manhandled into the building). The Waterside Restaurant also overlooks the marina and is painted a cool, elegant, pale green. There's a second dining room upstairs and a quieter bar at the back, the Captain's Lounge. The only disappointment is that the riverside terrace is so narrow, but there's not much the management can do about that!

Food is clearly the main business here, but the beer drinker is not forgotten with Greene King IPA, Adnams Bitter and Shepherd Neame Spitfire to choose from.

Lamb Hotel

2 Lynn Rd CB7 4EJ
Tel 01353 663574

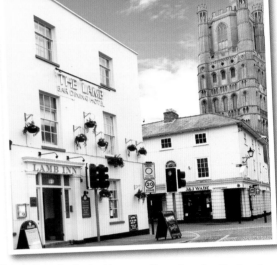

The survivor of the city's two principal coaching inns (the other was the Bell in the High Street, closed in 1960), the Lamb could be said to stand at the geographical centre of Ely. It's stood here for quite some time, too, since it's thought to be the inn recorded by Bishop Fordham in a survey of the Cathedral's property in 1416. However it doesn't first appear in the record-books as the Lamb until 1672, when it was mentioned in a will. In the 18th century its location on the crossroads in the middle of town propelled it to the status of principal inn, meeting place for the local turnpike trustees and the churchwardens of St Mary's.

AT A GLANCE

Opening times: 11-11 Mon-Sun. Food service: 11-2.30, 6-9 Mon-Fri; 12-9 Sat-Sun. Mains £6-£19.95. 31 letting rooms £20-£80. Small car park. No garden or patio. **Wheelchair access/disabled toilet**. Children and dogs welcome.

At that time it brewed its own beer; but when, in 1782, it was sold to Harlock's Brewery of Ely the brewhouse was turned into more stables and the maltings became a new coach-house. By 1828 the coaching trade was flourishing so mightily that the old buildings were demolished and replaced by the rather grand edifice you see today. The decline of coaching did nothing to diminish the Lamb's success: like many such old inns it became what was known as a "family and commercial hotel", using its stables and coach-house as the base for a horse-drawn omnibus service that met the trains at the station down by the river.

Today's Lamb is very much the upmarket meeting-place in Ely. Its smart bar, where real ales from Greene King are on tap, has leather sofas and stripped floorboards, with walls painted a tasteful peach and hung with photos and prints of local interest.

Minster Tavern

Minster Place CB7 4EL
Tel 01353 652900

The nearest pub to the Cathedral, the Minster Tavern goes back at least to 1817 when it was recorded as the Greyhound (becoming the Minster only in 1944). But although the present building, to judge by its symmetrical façade and sash windows, may be of about that date or somewhat earlier, the

cellars are much, much older. They comprise a series of vaults and chambers for all the world resembling monks' cells and the entrances to stopped-up tunnels, which has given rise to much speculation and supposition as well as tales of hauntings. Official histories of the cathedral don't mention any associated buildings on this site; but then Ely is so studded with medieval remnants that almost anything is feasible.

There's nothing medieval, though, about the bustling town-centre pub that exists today except, perhaps, its forest of fake beams. The big cheerful front bar has leather banquettes and a tiled floor; off to one side is a cosier area with comfortable armchairs, low ceilings, and a cosy-looking fireplace; at the back is a bright and sunny conservatory leading to a tiny patio for smokers. Beers are Marston's Pedigree, Shepherd Neame Spitfire, and Adnams Broadside.

The Prince Albert
62 Silver St CB7 4JF
Tel 01353 663494

Pubs may look pretty solid, but they do move. Well, their licences move, or did do in the days when the local authorities used to prevent what they called "proliferation" by operating a "one out, one in" system of granting new licences, which meant that when an old pub closed its licence was often transferred to a new one.

The Prince Albert is a case in point. The first mention of a pub of that name was in 1842, when its landlord

was charged with opening on a Sunday morning (ie, during the hours of divine service). It stood across the street from its present site; but in 1869 or thereabouts it closed and its licence was transferred to the newly-built Prince Albert you see today.

It still has something of a mid-Victorian air about it. It's not nearly as cluttered with bric-a-brac and paintings and ornaments and stuffed wildlife and so forth as any self-respecting Victorian parlour would have been; but it has a certain atmosphere of clerical respectability. The colour scheme of walls and upholstery is a restful, almost serene pale green; it's comfortably carpeted – none of your vulgar bare floorboards here – and through an archway off the L-shaped main bar is a cosy little side-room. This leads on in turn to a smokers' shelter and then a surprisingly big back garden that's a real suntrap on a summer's day.

A real drinkers' pub, the Prince Albert was the local Campaign for Real Ale pub of the year at time of writing and serves Greene King beers plus two guests. And although food isn't the real business, what food the pub does do it does extraordinarily well.

West End House
16 West End CB6 3AY
Tel 01353 662907

 Slightly out of the historic city centre, past Oliver Cromwell's House (aka the Tourist Information Office, but it really was Oliver Cromwell's house once), the West End House is down a side-street in an a quarter of mainly mid to late Victorian terraces. However the long, low, white-painted brick-built pub with its three dormers is clearly much older than its surroundings – and it's not the only building in the street that's a bit older than its surroundings, either: immediately across the road is an astonishing medieval stone hall or grange with high-peaked crow-stepped gables, now just a private house in a suburban avenue. Ely is that kind of place!

Originally two cottages (you can see where one of the front doors has been bricked up), it became a beer house in 1839, during the 30-year period when the 1830 Beer Act allowed householders to sell beer and cider (but not wines or spirits) without a justices' licence. In fact it didn't stop being a beer-only house until 1954, when a new landlord decided to apply for a full on-licence.

Although well off the main drag, the West End House is a must for visitors to Ely. Strictly speaking it's all one big bar, but it's all broken up into a jumble of odd corners and cosy nooks, including a delightful little snug off to one side. The décor is no-nonsense comfy: it's obviously old, but it doesn't make a song and dance about it. The same could be said for many of the regulars, who chaffer round the bar even on a chilly winter's morning in midweek.

A beer-drinker's pub, the West End House keeps Adnams Best and Shepherd Neame Spitfire as regulars, with up to three changing guest ales. You can eat here as well, though: there are baguettes for £3.50, ploughman's at £5, and – rather unexpected, this – tapas for £3.

The real find here, the icing on the cake, is the wonderful courtyard. Sheltered from the wind but not from the sun, the yard is all paved but is surrounded by beds and shrubs in pots and has not only a covered pergola for smokers but also, on the blank end wall of the house next door, a huge mural of (well, this is Ely) a medieval house.

AT A GLANCE
Opening times: 12-3, 6-11 Mon-Thurs; 12-12 Fri-Sat; 12-4, 7-11 Sun. Food service: 12-3. Occasional live music. Children welcome. Dogs in garden only.

Helpston

Bluebell
10 Woodgate PE6 7ED Tel 01733 252394

Few pubs trade on their literary connections as relentlessly as the Bluebell does – but then few pubs have a literary connection as strong as the Bluebell does. For John Clare, the "peasant poet", was born in the cottage next door in 1793, and his first proper job was as live-in potboy and general dogsbody at the Bluebell, where he stayed for a year before becoming a farm labourer. Hence the John Clare Snug and the Poet's Bar. But then the whole village trades on its association with Clare, who spent most of his life here and whose first major work was entitled "Helpstone" (it had a final "e" then; and the Bluebell was the Blue Bell then, changing its name only in 1993), so the pub's owners can be excused.

Having said that, the Bluebell's interior is the very antithesis of anything Clare would have recognised. Contemporary prints show the typical inn kitchen of Clare's day as being sparsely furnished to the point of severity, whereas the Bluebell's bar is a riot of ornament more like a late Victorian or Edwardian parlour. An exuberant mish-mash of furnishings includes an

unusual curved bench, upholstered in bright red and with a grandfather clock sticking up behind it, and an elaborate Edwardian-style overmantel

laden, as is every other flat surface in the place, with china animals and other sundry ornaments. Walls and rafters are hung with a marvellous miscellany of prints, mirrors, clocks, pewter tankards, brass toasting forks – anything, it seems, that can dangle from a nail. It's the perfect antidote, in short, to the epidemic of uncluttered cool that seems to have infected almost everywhere else.

But if the décor is calculated to raise a smile, the beer is serious here. Grainstore 1050 is an authentic recreation of the legendary Ruddle's County, from a brewery owned by the man who used to be Ruddle's head brewer. Grainstore also brews John Clare's Bitter exclusively for the Bluebell (you can buy bottles to take away as well as pints to drink on the premises). There are usually two guest ales; and in summer the pub also stocks two or three proper Herefordshire farmhouse ciders from Weston's.

Clare's cottage next door is undergoing heavy restoration as this book goes to press and is due to be reopened as a museum and educational centre by the John Clare Trust on July 13. Over the weekend of the reopening the John Clare Society (not to be confused with the Trust) will be holding a number of special events – and the Bluebell will be hosting a beer festival.

Holme

Admiral Wells
41 Station Rd PE7 3PH Tel 01487 831214 www.admiralwells.co.uk

Often, when I encounter a pub that was obviously built from scratch comparatively recently, I wonder what had previously been on the site. In this case, the answer is: the second biggest lake in England. For until 1852, when it was finally drained after 10 years of trying, this was Whittlesey Mere, a relic of primeval fen that the Dutch engineers who drained the rest of the region in the 17th century had somehow missed.

The improving landowner who planned, financed, and oversaw the disappearance of Whittlesey Mere, which had been second in size only to Windermere, was William Wells of Holmewood Hall; and when the work was done he first drove a couple of big iron posts all the way into the mud that had once been the mere's bed to measure its subsequent shrinkage, and then when the railway came through he built this pub next to the new station (now gone, of course) and named it after his grandfather.

The answer to your first question is that after 150 years of drying out and soil erosion, the posts now stand 13ft tall. The answer to your second is that Admiral Thomas Wells was a distinguished naval commander throughout the Revolutionary and Napoleonic wars and was one of the pall-bearers at Nelson's funeral after the Battle of Trafalgar.

So, not an ancient pub, but a handsome one nonetheless. It's not ancient inside, either: a thorough refurbishment of the lounge bar four or five years ago created a distinctly un-Victorian space of light and air, with stripped floorboards, pale wooden bar-fittings, and a rather elegant fireplace. The walls are hung with photographs and memorabilia commemorating the USAAF bomber crews stationed at nearby Glatton during the war. Round the corner from the lounge is a small and cosy snug. The dining-room is very smart and plush and leads on to a big sunny conservatory, also used for dining. There is also a functions room.

Well-known in the district for its food, the Admiral Wells attracts customers from a wide area and is almost always busy. But it has also long been celebrated for the range and quality of its cask beers. The regulars at present are Nethergate Augustinian, Digfield Shacklebush, and Wolf Brewery Bitter, and there are three constantly changing guests to boot.

A final mark of distinction is that standing on what was the bottom of Whittlesey Mere makes the Admiral Wells the lowest pub in Britain.

Parson Drove

Swan
Station Rd PE13 4HA Tel 01945 700291

A heathen place, Samuel Pepys called Parsons Drove when he came here on business in 1663; and where he stayed at "a miserable inne" – presumably this one, since there is no other. That night his uncle's horse was stolen from the inn stable, "at which I was inwardly glad that it was not mine"; so perhaps it was poetic justice that when he retired to his "sad, cold, nasty chamber" he ("and nobody else of our company, at which I wonder") was cruelly bitten by gnats.

Well, the Swan is no longer miserable, sad, nasty, or cold, but is cheerful, comfortable and warm, and is evidently much loved by the people of this "heathen place" since it supports a football team, a cricket team, a golf club, and an angling club. (As many as 80 anglers have been known to turn up for breakfast on a cold winter's morning).

Parts of the Swan were already old when Pepys briefly visited: the former smithy that makes up the rear wing (now the dining room) is said to have been built in 1541

of stone quarried from Crowland Abbey after its dissolution. The main block would have been newer: like so many coaching inns and posthouses, it was given a new symmetrical façade in the late 18th century, but the carcase of the building is more than a century older.

Very much the centre of community life, the Swan has something for everyone: as well as the dining room there's a cheerful bar with Elgood's beers on tap, a comfortable lounge, and a games room with bar billiards. Satellite TV shows the major sporting fixtures, and the food offering ranges from snacks to substantial meals at very reasonable prices. On the green that doubles as the

AT A GLANCE

Opening times:12-2.30, 5-11 Mon; 5-11 Tues-Wed; 12-2.30, 4.30-12 Thurs-Fri; 12-12 Sat; 12-11 Sun. Food service: 12-2, 5-8.30 Thurs-Mon; 5-8.30 Tues-Wed. Sandwiches etc £2.50-£3.75; mains £5-£9.99. Sunday carvery (summer), barbecue (winter). Car park. Children welcome. Dogs allowed in on leads.

pub garden in summer there's a structure known as the Cage, once the village lock-up and now housing a small but popular museum.

Peterborough

Brewery Tap

80 Westgate PE1 2AA Tel 01733 358500 www.oakham-ales.co.uk

Despite being under permanent threat of demolition for redevelopment, the Brewery Tap has been one of Peterborough's most popular pubs since it opened 11 years ago.

Once the town's Unemployment Benefit Office, the big 1930s building became the home of Oakham Ales in 1998 after a long planning battle during which it emerged that the whole site including the Greene King pub next door was scheduled to make way for an extension to the enormous Queensgate Shopping Centre across the street. Work has been postponed again and again for one reason and another, the recession being the cause of the latest reprieve; but although the

Greene King pub closed as soon as the plan was published and has remained closed ever since, neither Oakham Ales nor the Brewery Tap have let their permanent condition of blight hold them back. The brewery has recently moved to a big new site outside the city centre; but there's still a working brewing plant on show behind huge glass panels at the Tap, which is buzzing as if there was no tomorrow – which, of course, there might not be.

AT A GLANCE

Opening times: 12-11 Sun-Thurs; 12-1am Fri-Sat. Food service: 12-2.30, 6-9.30 Sun-Thurs; 12-10.30 Fri-Sat. Snacks etc £1.59-£8.49. Mains £5.99-£6.99. Big-screen TV (terrestrial only). No car park, patio, or garden. Children welcome during food service. Dogs allowed in bar. **Wheelchair access/disabled toilet.**

A cavernous and very modern bar is split up by partitions and sundry other decorative devices into separate areas, some of them equipped with deep leather sofas, while there's also a big mezzanine floor for dining (the food is Thai, well-priced, and excellent) and a functions room. At least five of Oakham's own ales are always on tap, along with Elgood's Black Dog, two draught ciders from Weston's, and up to six guest ales. There's also a superb collection of bottled Belgian beers. But don't let this embarrassment of beery riches leads you to think that this is some sort of CAMRA ghetto: the live DJs on Friday and Saturday nights play to large and varied crowds, some with sandals and beer-bellies, most without.

Charters Bar

Town Bridge PE1 1EH
Tel 01733 315700
www.charters-bar.co.uk
www.bluesontheboat.co.uk

If you thought an old dole office was an unlikely home for an upscale beer bar, how about a century-old Dutch grain barge? But Oakham Ales owner Paul Hook evidently has an eye for the unusual; and the Brewery Tap's sister-pub is if anything even more idiosyncratic.

The 176-ft Leendert-R, as the barge was known in its first incarnation, shipped grain, sand, and gravel around the inland waterways of Holland, Belgium, and Germany from 1907 until 1990, when Paul bought it and shipped it across the North Sea, finally bringing it to rest – not without difficulty, given the height of the bridge it had to squeeze under – at its present moorings in the Nene just outside the city centre.

Like the Tap, Charters is a living expression of Paul's twin passions: oriental food and fine beer.

On the main decks is a restaurant, East, offering cuisines from all points east of the Indus. Meanwhile the hold, which once held over 600 tonnes of cargo, has been transformed into a vast bar where 12 handpumps dispense Oakham's own ales plus guests and up to four Weston's traditional ciders. The bottled Belgian beers fill two fridges. You can order Thai-inspired bar snacks including a Thai burger, or have full meals sent down from the restaurant above. On Friday and Saturday nights Charters becomes not only one of Peterborough's best

AT A GLANCE
Opening times:
12-11 Mon-Thurs;
12-2am Fri-Sat;
12-10.30 Sun.
Food service:
12-2.30, 5-10.
Thai bar snacks
£4.95-£5.95.

beer bars but also one of its hottest music venues, when live bands take to the tiny stage for blues and r'n'b sessions.

Perhaps surprisingly, Charters also boasts what is thought to be the city's biggest beer garden complete with an enormous gazebo for smokers. Four times a year the gazebo's folding sides are rolled down, wooden stillages are rolled in, and the smokers are rolled out for beer festivals.

Coalheavers Arms
5 Park St, Woodston PE2 9BH
Tel 01733 565664
www.individualpubs.co.uk

An unassuming backstreet local in a quiet quarter of Victorian and Edwardian terraces just outside the city centre, the Coalheavers Arms has become something of a beer-lover's paradise since the Individual Pub Company – sister-company to Cambridge's Milton Brewery – took it over in 2002. The counter in its single big stone-flagged bar mounts eight handpumps dispensing three Milton beers, Mole's Black Rat Cider, and up to four guest ales, and its long, narrow, secluded garden hosts spring and autumn beer festivals which have become legendary almost as much for their live music and tug o' war as for the beer. They like dressing up, here, too, especially at the Hallowe'en and New Year's Eve parties which are just about as legendary as the beer festivals.

AT A GLANCE
Opening times:
5-11 Mon-Wed;
12-2, 5-11 Thurs;
12-11 Fri-Sat;
12-10.30 Sun.
Wifi/internet access. Smoking shelter in garden. Children allowed until early evening and at weekends. Dogs welcome.

Being a beer-drinker's pub, the Coalheavers doesn't go big on food. You can get a sandwich pretty much throughout opening times ranging in price from an incredibly modest £1.80 to a scarcely less modest £3, but be warned: the £3 sandwiches are enormous. You may want to share.

Palmerston Arms

82 Oundle Rd PE2 9PA
Tel 01733 565865

Just a stone's throw from the Coalheavers if you
know the short cut – and not much further if you
don't – is yet another of the beer-lover's paradises
which make living in Peterborough more than bear-
able.

Before sampling the ale at the Palmerston Arms,
though, take a second look at its exterior. On a busy
thoroughfare through a fairly run-down area of Victorian terraces, it shares the corners of a little crossroads
with a sex shop and a tattoo and piercing parlour. But
the pub itself belongs to a different world: it's no brick-
built Victorian street-corner local but an 18th-century
cottage of local stone, a survival from the days when
Oundle Road was a country lane, and looking very out
of place amid the urban unpleasantness that surrounds
it.

Inside, it's an absolute gem still divided into a very
traditional quarry-tiled public bar and a slightly more
upmarket lounge (it's got a carpet). Actually, the current layout is quite recent: the pub has no cellar and
no handpumps, and all the beers are drawn direct from
barrels mounted on stillages in a cold-room. Until three or
four years ago the stillage room was tucked away down a

corridor at the back, out of sight of
the customers; but then the pub's

AT A GLANCE

Opening times:
3-11 Mon-Wed;
3-12 Thurs-Fri;
12-12 Sat; 12-11
Sun. Wifi/internet
access. Covered
patio for smokers.
Children until
early evening.
Dogs welcome.

owner, Lincolnshire family brewer
Bateman's, rejigged the interior so
that the stillages became visible
through a glass panel behind the bar. The reconstruction also had the ef-
fect of creating more space for drinkers, so good on Bateman's.

Good on Bateman's, too, for not operating a strict tie (not that a Bateman's tie is a bad thing). In fact only three of the beers usually come from
Wainfleet; the rest (typically five during the week and twice that at weekends) are ever-changing guests from other brewers large and small – but
mostly small.

One tip: eat before you get here. The pub has no kitchen, all the available space being taken up by the stillages, and does no food at all.

Wortley Almshouses

Westgate PE1 1QA Tel 01733 348839

Surely the handsomest building on Westgate, the Wortley Almshouses is a relic not from
1837, as the datestone over the door suggests, but from nearly a century earlier. It was actually a gift to the city (or more likely a bribe to the handful of property owners then entitled
to vote) from its MP, Sir Edward Wortley Montague, in 1744, and was first used as a workhouse. However by the 1830s it was far too small for the number of paupers it was expected
to accommodate; so a new workhouse was found and Sir Edward's gift was reinvented as

a row of almshouses. The 1837 date probably refers to the rather collegiate mock-Tudor stone façade, which looks as if it had been added at that time.

The building was bought for conversion into a pub nearly 30 years ago by the Yorkshire family brewer Sam Smith's during one of its expansionist phases (it has another pub in Peterborough, the Botolph in Oundle Road, and others in Stamford and Bourn); but in its first incarnation it is said to have been a rather barn-like open-plan affair.

Then in 2003 Sam's decided to gut the place completely, stripping it right back to the original brick floors and uncovering an original fireplace in the process, and to redesign it to be more in keeping with its historic role. Hence today's arrangement of six rooms, all laid out in line like the compartments on and old-fashioned train. Some of these rooms are tiny, only big enough for a single table with a fixed bench on each side; others are spacious by comparison. The subdued lighting and colour-scheme, the absence of music, the lack of clutter, and the dignified prints of various Wortley Montagues, all make for a calm, studious, reflective atmosphere which won the Best Refurbishment category in the Campaign for Real Ale's 2004 Pub Design Awards.

Sam's is something of an eccentric company: it produces only one cask beer, Old Brewery Bitter, whose price it hold down as ruthlessly as it can: at £1.52 a pint it's a real Yorkshire bargain. For variety, though, the company also produces an enormous range of excellent if pricey bottled beers, all on sale here, and rather than allowing Guinness into its pubs produces its own draught stout, also on sale here.

AT A GLANCE

Opening times:
12-11 Mon-Sat;
12-5.30 Sun.
Food service:
12-2 Mon-Sat.
Light meals and sandwiches £2.50-£3.95.
Mains and grills £4.50-£7.50.

Stilton

Bell

Great North Rd PE7 3RA   Tel 01733 241066
www.thebellstilton.co.uk

One of the greatest delights the country has to offer to any connoisseur of grand old inns is the Bell at Stilton, famous the world over for its antiquity, for its extravagant wrought-iron inn-sign, and for its place as the cradle of Stilton cheese. And any first-time visitor with any sympathy at all for old inns will approach the Bell with at least some trepidation: does it live up to its billing?

Well, I can tell them: yes it does, and then some.

But first, the cheese. It's always said that Stilton cheese was first popularised by Cooper Thornhill, dashing equestrian extraordinaire (holder of the Stilton-London speed record), who ran the Bell from 1730-1759 and used to pass off blue cheese he sourced from Leicestershire to his customers as local produce. This was despite the fact that the white cheese made in Stilton itself had been well-known even before Thornhill's day (Daniel Defoe, writing in the 1720s, commented rather gloomily that "our English Parmesan" came crawling with mites, which you were expected to eat with the spoon provided). So that's the cheese story. The Bell's own story is more remarkable yet.

AT A GLANCE
Opening times: 12-2.30, 6-11 Mon-Thurs; 12-2.30, 6-12 Fri; 12-2, 6-12 Sat; 12-3, 7-11 Sun. Food service: 12-2.15, 6-9.30 Mon-Fri; 12-2.30, 6-9.30 Sat; 12-2.30 7-9 Sun. Mains £10.25-£16.45 (bistro); three courses £29.95 (restaurant). Car park; courtyard patio, garden. 22 letting rooms: £73.50 (single) to £130.50 (four-poster). Children welcome in dining-rooms during the day **Wheelchair access/disabled toilet.**

It was first recorded as an inn in the early 16th century, although the buildings you see are mid-17th; and it was extended in the mid-18th century to capture the passing trade on the Great North Road, although the Angel opposite was the main coaching inn. When coaches gave way to trains the Bell fell on hard times and was divided into three tenements, one of which remained as an alehouse and one of which became the residence of a Roman Catholic bishop and was therefore officially a palace. In the mid-1970s the pub closed, and was completely derelict until the mid-'80s when it was bought by an Essex man of Irish extraction, Liam McGivern.

He had made his money in Saudi Arabia and proceeded to pour it into buying and restoring the Bell, an enormous and even heroic undertaking since nothing original was left save the façade and the fireplaces. A single bar was ready for reopening in 1990 (local MP John Major cutting the ribbon); but for many years after that it was a work in progress, the bistro not being ready to open until 2003. But to tour the place with its warren of bars, parlours, snugs and galleried dining-room you wouldn't guess that it was a restoration, so skilfully has the work been done. Even the immense wrought-iron gallows sign is a recreation of the original. Just sit in the Village Bar in winter beside the great fire that burns 3,000-year-old bog oak logs, and with a pint of ale (Greene King IPA and Abbot, Digfied Barnwell Bitter, Fuller's London Pride and a changing guest) in your hand, and you could almost be back in Cooper Thornhill's day, waiting for the horses on your post-chaise to be changed.

Stretham

Lazy Otter
Elford Close CB6 3LU Tel 01353 649780

Although never a coaching inn, the Lazy Otter owes its existence to the growth of the coaching trade in the 18th century which led to the turnpiking of the Roman road from Cambridge to King's Lynn (Akeman Street or, in more modern parlance, the A10). Akeman Street had fallen into disuse centuries before, and throughout the medieval period the main north-south route was via Aldreth, several miles to the west, where there was a causeway across the Great Ouse which has now entirely disappeared (although there is still a ford).

Here at Elford Close just south of Stretham there was only a ferry until 1763, when the local turnpike trust built a bridge that created, for the first time in several centuries, a continuous road link between Cambridge and Ely and soon succeeded in capturing the traffic that had previously used the Aldreth Causeway.

Today's Lazy Otter first entered the record books in 1797 as a wayside alehouse called the Royal Oak, which was by then, according to one writer, already "old and well-established". The bridge at whose foot it stood was had been built so high to let barges pass under it that farm carts had to have extra horses hitched to get across it – thirsty work that no doubt called for a few beers. Nevertheless it remained until 1925, when the present bridge was built and tested by having four steam traction engines parked on it.

All this time the Royal Oak had been dutifully and mostly uneventfully (save for a disastrous fire in 1844, after which it was completely rebuilt) serving the stream of passing trade that used Akeman Street. Then in 1976 the main road was widened and realigned over a new bridge, and the pub found itself marooned on a little loop road. The new situation called for a rethink, and in 1986 the Royal Oak was closed and virtually rebuilt, re-emerging in 1987 with a new name (although some people still use the old one), a marina of its own, and a mission to begin a new life exploiting its beautiful riverside setting.

In this it has succeeded. Cambridgeshire has many riverside pubs, and the Lazy Otter can hold its head up among the best of them. Very smart inside, its stripped and varnished floorboards, leather armchairs and sofas, Victorian-style fireplaces, and airy riverfront dining room create an atmosphere of relaxed affluence that makes it a difficult place to leave.

Red Lion
47 High St CB6 3JQ
Tel 01353 648123

In the very heart of the village, next to St Michael's Church and with the 15th-century village cross (described by the Victoria County History as Cambridgeshire's "most perfect surviving example") right outside its front door, the Red Lion is an ivy-clad 18th-century posthouse with a comforting solidity and sense of place about it.

The reassuring air con-
tinues into the smart and
uncluttered public bar with
its scattering of old photographs, muted Farrow &
Ball colour-scheme, and
efficient-looking wood-
burning stove. The lounge
is, as a lounge should be,
a notch or two higher on
the plush scale; and there's
also a big carpeted con-
servatory dining room.

Food is important here,
but new licensee is working hard to make sure that the Red Lion remains
as attractive to drinkers as to diners and continues to serve as the bustling
social hub of its own community. So if all the food is sourced from local
producers/suppliers (the herbs come from a small roof-garden, and it
doesn't come more local than that!) and freshly cooked on the premises,
there are still very well-priced offers such as pie and a pint for £5 alongside five real ales – Greene King IPA, Adnams Bitter and Broadside, and
guests from local micros) – and Sky TV and a dartboard in the public bar.

Sutton-in-the-Isle

Anchor
Sutton Gault,
Sutton
CB6 2BD
Tel 01353 778537
www.anchorsut
tongault.
co.uk

**One of the best-
known dining
pubs in this part of
Cambridgeshire, the
Anchor stands right
next to the New
Bedford River, one**
of the arrow-straight watercourses created to drain the fens in the mid-17th century. The
pub claims the same date as the river having been built, supposedly, to house the Scottish
prisoners captured after the Battle of Dunbar in 1650, who provided the labour that dug the
channel. Rather alarmingly, given the age of the embankment that holds the waters in their
course, the Anchor is well below the level of the river. One hopes that the Scots built well!

However, it's an unlikely if familiar tale. Many village inns are said to have been built to house
the masons who built the parish church; in every case I know of the supposed lodging is several
centuries younger than the church. The same is true of the two clearly Victorian London pubs said

to have been provided to house the labour force working on St Paul's Cathedral. At least in this case the two events are roughly coincidental; but given that 3,600 of the 5,000 Scottish prisoners captured at Dunbar died of hunger and ill-treatment on their brutal forced march south, it seems unlikely that anyone would have gone to the trouble to provide them with so much as a tent, let alone such a handsome little place as the Anchor.

And make no mistake, the Anchor is handsome. Its four rooms, arranged in a long row, are tasteful in the extreme, with original fireplaces, golden oak beams unsmeared by the near-ubiquitous pitch, floors of polished tiles, and elegant panelled walls. It is, in short, the perfect place in which to enjoy the standard of cuisine (described as modern British with influences from around the world, and all made with fresh, local, and seasonal ingredients) for which it is renowned; the sort of place that makes you feel rich even if you're not.

Ufford

White Hart
Main St PE9 3BH
Tel 01780 740250

An unassuming sort of place from outside, the White Hart's unspectacular frontage conceals many surprises.

The first, and perhaps least surprising – least surprising because it's been there for five years – is that there's a brewery in the little old barn in the car park. Ufford Ales supplies the White Hart and five other pubs in the same ownership as well as a handful of local free houses and beer festivals.

The second surprise is that the pub's commitment to localism doesn't stop at the ale. Owner Michael Thurlby farms in nearby Tallington, and virtually all the lamb, pork and poultry on the menu comes from his own and neighbouring farms. There are plans to run some of the sheep and pigs

on the pub's own land, which will make the meat more local still.

Finally, there's the décor. You expect a 17th-century country pub to be rustic, but the bar at the White Hart is so full-on rustic you half expect to see Sid behind the bar and Eddie and Joe trying to cadge a free pint of Shire's. The walls have been stripped right back to bare stone; the floor is of huge flagstones; you could spit-roast half a pig in the fireplace; from the exposed rafters hang fearsome agricultural imple-ments including a lethal-looking hay knife, a sharp-pointed peat spade, and a dairymaid's yoke; there's also a collection of china gazunders that must be of national importance; and the walls are adorned with various signs rescued from the local railway line when it was Beechinged.

The dining room, it has to be admitted, is much more refined, although it too has bare stone walls and an enormous fireplace; while the conserva-tory that links the main body of the pub to the old stables (now a func-tions suite) is almost fairy-tale by contrast with its candy-stripe hangings, cream-coloured wicker chairs, and écru carpet (or is it taupe?).

Wansford

Paper Mills
London Rd
PE8 6JB
Tel 01780 782328

In any other setting, the Paper Mills would be regarded as rather an elevated establishment. In Wansford, however, it is somewhat overshadowed by its majestic neighbour. For those overawed by the Haycock's grandeur, though, the humbler Paper Mills is an altogether less intimidating (and less expensive) alternative.

Named after the mills that occupied the rear of the site until the mid-19th century, the handsome stone-built pub doubles as a dining-house of some distinction and also one of two village locals, the real ales being Greene King IPA and Abbot and a guest. The big open-plan bar is deco-rated in the style of a gentrified cottage parlour, while the smart dining room leads through to a bright, sunny conservatory. Beyond is a garden that within living memory gave on to the riverbank but now, perhaps sadly, has a house on it.

Haycock

London Road PE8 6JA.
Tel 01780 782223.
www.thehaycock.co.uk

Millions of motorists driving north along the A1 will have glimpsed the back of the Haycock and perhaps realised what an enormous establishment it is. So enormous, in fact, with its 48 bedrooms, its ballroom, its restaurants, private dining rooms, conservatory, meeting rooms, formal gardens, sheds, barns and heaven knows what else that you might question whether it should be included in a pub guide at all.

Well, it does have a public bar, open to non-residents and non-diners and with three real ales (Adnams Bitter, Bass, Fuller's Chicwick), albeit very civilised, albeit rather tucked away, and albeit called a cocktail bar; but this corner of the massive rambling mountain of masonry at least qualifies as a pub. And it calls itself an inn, rather than a hotel, so perhaps a point may be stretched.

Besides, the Haycock is so significant as the most palatial of the Great North Road's coaching inns that it's simply impossible to omit. The bridge over the Nene, at whose foot it stands, is the latest in a succession going back to the early 13th century, and an inn called sometimes the Swan and sometimes the White Swan is recorded in 1571 but was probably there for three centuries before that, odd and ends of medieval fabric having been uncovered during various phases of extension and rebuilding.

By the 1630s, the coaching trade using the bridge had become so lucrative that the old Swan was completely rebuilt in the classical style then being popularised by Inigo Jones. It was renamed, too, in the late 17th or early 18th century, after a comic ballad recounting the adventures of Drunken Barnaby who fell asleep on a haybale which was washed down the Nene in a flash flood.

...People cried
as along the stream I hied:
'Whither away?' quoth they, 'from Greenland?'
'No, from Wansford Bridge, in England!'

(The conceit being that the flood had washed him over the county boundary into that corner of Lincolnshire then known as Holland).

The new inn was built on a grand scale. Behind its plain but dignified and, indeed, enormous stone façade lay a complex of noble apartments, servants' lodgings, kitchens, storerooms, stables staffed by 20 ostlers, lofts, brewery, and barns all reputedly roofed by more an acre of Colly-weston stone, as well as formal gardens, kitchen garden, paddocks and hayfields extending to 625 acres.

It certainly succeeded in capturing the upper echelon of the trade, too, with every celebrity from Princess Victoria down choosing it as the best place to overnight during its 250-year career. But when steam succeeded horsepower it could only struggle along, finally closing in 1887. Then petrol succeeded steam, and in 1928 it was reopened. It has never looked back.

So, maybe more palace than pub. But call in for a pint anyway, just to say you have.

AT A GLANCE

Opening times (cocktail bar): 11-11 seven days. Restaurant open 12-2.30, 6.30-9.30 Mon-Sat; 12-3 Sun. Sandwiches available 24 hours. Afternoon teas. Brasserie menu £6.95-£10.50. Sandwiches, snacks and tapas £4.50-£6.95. Set lunch £14.50 (2 courses). Sunday lunch £19.95 (3 courses). À la carte mains £13.95-£16.95. Bedrooms/suites £90-£210. Extensive gardens. Families welcome. **Wheelchair access/disabled toilets**.

Red Lion
32 North Brink PE13 1JR

Tel 01954 582022

The term "flagship pub" is an invidious one. Not only does it give the tenant concerned a lot to live up to, it also sets all the other tenants wondering what he/she's got that they haven't. But since the Red Lion is the nearest pub to its parent brewery, Elgood's, and since the head brewer himself drinks there – well, if the cap fits...

North Brink is definitely the posh end of Wisbech, with a row of handsome Georgian and Victorian town houses that includes the National Trust-owned Peckover House with its two acres of formal gardens. But further along North Brink, between Peckover House and the brewery, is a stretch of humbler buildings, all of much the same late Georgian date but once the homes of the shopkeepers and trades-men who made their living by supplying their grander neighbours. Small pubs that catered to these shopkeepers and tradesmen, as well as to the servants of the well-off, are common fea-tures of the older quarters of our towns and cities, so it's not an unreasonable assumption that this was the purpose the Red Lion originally served.

But if it ever was the exclusive haunt of the humbler classes, it certainly isn't now. Originally three bars (and in servants' pubs these bars were often hierarchically stratified as rigidly as the messes in a barracks, so that no footman would dare drink in the butlers' bar), it's all been knocked into one light, airy, uncluttered room, long and narrow and with some original features, especially the fireplace which is the only place where horse-brasses are permitted to show them-selves. Otherwise the décor is restrained and includes a few original watercolours by a local artist.

The split-level dining room is a recent addition, created by the conversion of an old barn and very smart indeed.

AT A GLANCE
Opening times: 11.30-2.30, 6-11 Mon-Fri; 12-3, 7-11.30 Sat; 12-3, 7-11 Sun. Food service: 12-2, 7-9. Baguettes £3.95. Mains £6.95-£14.95. Car park. Patio and court-yard. Children in dining room only. **Wheelchair access/disabled toilet**.

Abbotsley

Eight Bells
High St PE19 6UJ
Tel 01767 677305

Abbotsley is a picturesque and well-heeled village in the rolling countryside east of St Neots whose affluent citizens have high expectations of their locals. But they've had an unhappy time with their two pubs in recent years. The Jolly Abbot unaccountably switched from high-end dining, which was very popular, to big-screen TV sports, which wasn't. It remains firmly closed. At the same time the Eight Bells was hit by a disastrous fire and was itself closed for six months. Now, though, the Eight Bells is back on track after a very sympathetic refurbishment by owner Greene King. Originally three cottages, it has a big L-shaped split-level bar with just enough beams and horse-brasses to signify

its age but not so many as to brag about it, and a separate dining-room divided from the bar by a big open fireplace. The décor is contemporary and comfortable – carpets and upholstery rather than bare boards and benches – and light and airy, taking full advantage of the pub's west-facing aspect that lets the sun flood in.

But the pub's chief glory is its big back garden, which looks out over a broad shallow valley to the hilly woodland beyond. "Eight bells" is naval terminology for 5 o' clock, or knocking off time, which is why so many pubs bear the name. And once you have knocked off, the garden at the Eight Bells in Abbotsley is the perfect place for an early evening sundowner or, on warm nights, an alfresco dinner.

AT A GLANCE
Opening times: 5.30-11 Mon; 12-3, 5.30-11 Tues-Thurs; 12-3, 5.30-12 Fri; 12-12 sat; 12-11 Sun. Food service 12-2.30, 6-9 Tues-sat; 12-3 Sun. Mains £7.50-£10.95. Wifi/internet access. **Wheelchair access/disabled toilet**. Covered patio. Big car park. Children and dogs welcome.

Abbots Ripton

Three Horsehoes
Moat Lane PE28 2PA
Tel 01487 773440
www.thethreehorseshoes.com

The Three Horseshoes is an achingly pretty but absolutely tiny 17th-century thatched cottage that was probably once the village blacksmith's forge. The ceilings in its two little rooms – a cosy snug and an elegant dining-room – are so low that the beams will brush the head of a person of only modest height.

But then – isn't the Three Horseshoes a big, brand-new pub, built only in 2004, with a very plush bar, an opulent restaurant, and six luxurious letting rooms?

Well, of course, it's both. But the original pub, which must surely have been one of the smallest in the county, actually closed down in 1998, leaving the villagers of Abbots Ripton with no facilities. Then the Abbots Ripton Estate got to work regenerating the village, which it mostly owns, building a brand-new village hall, reopening the shop and post office, and effectively adding an entirely new pub to the old alehouse. It's a marriage that works; and if the older part somehow seems like an extension of the newer part rather than vice versa – well, it's a very charming extension.

The pub is, of course, much too big for the village. But its reputation for good food ensures a steady stream of eager diners, attracted by a menu all freshly-made on the premises from the cream of local suppliers (and there are quite a few very high-end producers in this affluent corner of the world). The beer has its fans, too: the handpumps on the bar are dummies and the ales (Woodforde Wherry, Adnams Bitter, Fuller's London Pride, Oakham JHB and two guests) are all kept on stillage.

Alconbury Weston

White Hart
2 Vinegar Hill PE28 4JA Tel 01480 890331

It hardly seems possible, but when the White Hart was built in the 17th century, the Great North Road actually passed its front door, and for the first 200 years of its existence coaches, post-chaises and waggons thundered by like the traffic on today's A1(M) a few hundred yards across the fields to the east.

I say "thundered by" because most of it did, without stopping. The greater inns where the stage-coaches and mails stopped to change horses were at Buckden and Brampton to the south and Stilton and Wansford to the north; but Alconbury Weston was halfway up the long, weary, highwayman-infested haul from Alconbury to Alconbury Hill, where the Great North Road and Ermine street met (and where the gibbet stood); and plenty of drivers of private coaches and

AT A GLANCE
Opening times: 12-2.30-5.30-11 Mon-Fri; 12-4, 6.30-11 Sat; 12-5.30 Sun. Food service: 12-2, 6-9 Mon-Thurs; 12-2, 6-9.30 Fri; 12-2, 7-9.30 sSt; 12-2 Sun. Mains £8-£12.80. Lunchtime menu £5.50. Children's menu £5. Small car park.. Garden. Smoking shelter. No dogs during food service.

post-chaises would have been glad to pause at the White Hart to water their horses – and no doubt, themselves.

Well, there's not much passing trade in Alconbury Weston any more; but with a range of ales including Adnams Bitter, Courage Directors, and two guests (and its spring and autumn beer and cider festivals), with its well-priced menu, its garden, its occasional live music, and its petanque court, it does sterling duty as a well-rounded village local.

And with its oak beams, its big brick fireplace dividing bar from parlour, and its twin bay windows where travellers would sit and watch for their coaches, the venerable White Hart still has something of the glory days about it.

Boxworth

Golden Ball
High Street CB3 8LY
Tel 01954 267379
www.goldenballhotel.co.uk

Until 10 or so years ago, the Golden Ball was no more than a little pub in a little village, pretty enough with its white-washed walls and thatched roof, but otherwise undistinguished. Then its owner, the Bedford brewer Charles Wells, went mad and grafted on to the 17th-century cottage a series of extensions that dwarfs the original.

But the marriage is a happy one, and unites a new block comprising big, sunny, spacious, bar boasting a feature bare-brick fireplace, tapestries hanging from the high ceiling, and comfy-looking leather armchairs, with, in the old part, the cutest little dining room you ever saw. There's another, much bigger and very plush dining room too, of course – the old one couldn't accommodate a quarter of the people who flock to what is, after all, a fairly remote pub. But the food here is a powerful magnet, with a well-priced menu comprising 60 or 70 different dishes, all of them freshly made from local ingredients.

There are also letting rooms in yet another new block – the place calls itself the Golden Ball Hotel these days – and a large, beautifully-maintained, and generously-equipped garden. Real ales are Charles Wells Eagle and Bombardier and two guests.

Broughton

Crown
Bridge Road PE28 3AY
Tel 01487 824428
www.thecrowninnrestaurant.
co.uk

Another of those Cambridgeshire pubs like the Dyke's End at Reach and the Pig & Abbot at Abington Piggotts that had to be rescued by its own locals, the Crown had been peacefully pulling pints for nearly 250 years (and for quite a large part of that time selling saddlery as well) when suddenly Big Business intervened.

In the 1960s the Crown fell victim to Watney's invasion of East Anglia, when the country's (if not the world's) most hated brewing company snapped up all three of Norfolk's old-established breweries – to one or other of which the pub belonged – almost in one bite. Then in 1988 the pub was one of a big tranche sold by Watney's to a property company, which later sold out to another property company, which in 2000 showed its true colours by trying to sell the Crown as a private house. This was perhaps understandable in a highly

Opening times:
Closed Mon-Tues.
11.30-3, 6.30-11
Wed-Sat; 11-6
Sun. Food service:
12-2.30, 7-10
Wed-Sat; 12-2.30
Sun. Lunch spe-
cials £11.50-£14.
Sunday set lunch
£14.50-£17. À la
carte mains £9.50-
£15.50. Large
car park. Patio.
Huge garden.
Children welcome:
small portions on
request. Dogs
allowed.

favoured village where a handsome and spacious late 18th or early 19th century building with a very large garden indeed (big enough for a separate building plot?) would be worth far more as a very des des res than as a pub. The villagers, however, realised that their own des reses would be a lot less des without a watering hole; so 44 of them put their hands in their pockets and quickly produced the £180,000 necessary to buy it for themselves.

Reopening in 2001 with the former chef from the Old Bridge Hotel, Huntingdon, as tenant, the Crown was an instant hit mainly for the quality of its food, which lured gastronauts from far and wide.

A year ago the village consortium sold the pub on to an investment company, which has changed very little other than the chef-tenant. Despite its age, the pub has an open, airy, sunny interior with a cool decorative scheme of white and eau de nil painted walls, tiled floors, and pitch-pine bar-fittings and furniture. It's a wine-drinker's pub rather than a beer-drinker's pub, although it does keep Greene King IPA and a guest ale on handpump. The food on offer is described as British, but with French and Italian influences. Chef-patron David Anderton sources everything as locally as possible – the fruit and veg mostly come all the way from Bedfordshire, but the potatoes come from a farm in Broughton itself, while the pigeons, when in season, are supplied by a bloke who turns up at the back door with the day's bag. Now that's local!

Buckden

George Hotel
Old Great North Road, PE19 5XA
Tel: 01480 812300
www.thegeorgebuckden.com

A huge and imposing brick-built 18th-century coaching inn, the George fronts what used to be the Great North Road until the affluent village of Buckden was bypassed by the A1 in the 1960s. In its glory days the George was a staging post for the York Flyer and the landlord, a man named Cartwright, drove the Welwyn-Buckden stage of 70 miles himself.

Despite, or perhaps because of, its size, the end of the coaching era hit the George hard: half of it was sold off as shops – one of them the village post office – and the half that stayed in business as a hotel gradually declined both in status and standards.

Then in 2003 it was bought by the Furbank family, who had already acquired the shops in the other half of the old building one by one and turned them into a single very swish dress-shop with a reputation across East Anglia and beyond. An extremely expensive refurbishment transformed the George into a thoroughly modern and very stylish bar and brasserie, very cool and contemporary, with scarcely a trace of the era of coach-horn and blunderbuss left (although the Reading Room, a small private meeting or dining room, has a certain Georgian elegance about it). Indeed, the Orangery bistro is positively Mediterranean in its style and décor.

That, and the high-end fine dining, doesn't deter the villagers from dropping into the bar for a pint, though, with real ales from Nethergate and Adnams always in dependable condition.

There are also 12 luxury bedrooms all named after various Georges including Best, Orwell, and Harrison as well as conference facilities and a functions suite.

Lion
Old Great North Rd
PE19 5XA
Tel 01480 810313

A greater contrast with the ultra-modernised George than the Lion immediately opposite could scarcely be imagined. Where the George is and looks 18th century, the Lion is much, much older. It is reliably attested as far back as 1492, when it was the Bishop of Lincoln's guest-house. Buckden Towers, just next door to the Lion and village's outstanding landmark, was one of the Bishop's residences both before and after the Reformation; and while many monastic guest-houses became privately-owned inns after their parent houses were dissolved, the Lion long remained the property of the diocese.
A memory of the inn's

ecclesiastical origins and ownership is preserved in the wooden boss
that holds together the extraordinary fan of beams in the bar ceiling: it is
carved in the form of a lamb and flag, and around it are engraved in Gothic
lettering the words "ecce agnus dei", behold the Lamb of God. And when
it became a commercial inn, its name was indeed the Lamb & Flag, before
it contracted merely to the Lamb and was then expanded again with the
addition of a lion taken from the diocesan coat of arms. So it remained
until the late 19th century, when the lamb finally disappeared completely
from the inn sign.

ecclesiastical origins and ownership is preserved in the wooden boss
that holds together the extraordinary fan of beams in the bar ceiling: it is
carved in the form of a lamb and flag, and around it are engraved in Gothic
lettering the words "ecce agnus dei", behold the Lamb of God. And when
it became a commercial inn, its name was indeed the Lamb & Flag, before
it contracted merely to the Lamb and was then expanded again with the
addition of a lion taken from the diocesan coat of arms. So it remained
until the late 19th century, when the lamb finally disappeared completely
from the inn sign.

Inside, too, the Lion and the George could not be more different. Where
the George has gone ultra-modern, the Lion has remained a genteel and
gentrified hotel of the traditional kind with its comfortably scuffed soft
furnishings, its black oak beams, its great formal fireplaces, and its dignified dark panelled walls unaccountably hung with prints of French coats of
arms. Not a place for a night out with the lads, despite the choice of up to
three cask beers mainly from Adnams and Woodforde's.

AT A GLANCE

Opening times:
11-11 Mon-Sat;
12-10.30 Sun.
Food service:
12-2.30, 6.30-9.
Mains £6.95-
£17.95. Wifi/
internet access.
14 letting rooms:
£50 single, £80
double. Car park.
Small terrace.
Children welcome.

Catworth

Fox
Fox Lane
PE28 0PW
Tel 01832 710363

**Anyone who's ever
driven westward from
Huntingdon along the
A14 – which must be
pretty well everyone
– knows the Fox at
least by sight: it's so
close to the road that
a nearside passenger
could virtually reach
out of the window
and touch it, and it
has the words "Fox
Food" painted in 6ft
letters on its roof. But
seeing it is not quite
the same as reach-
ing it: to do that,
you have to exit the**

**A14 on to the B660, signposted Catworth, and just over the bridge heading south there a
sliproad on your right which leads you to the Fox.**

The detour is well worth it, for the Fox is a proper gem of an old-fashioned country pub (built in
the 1840s, but on a site where an alehouse had stood for at least a century before that), unself-
conscious and workaday with its white-painted walls, its scattering of black beams, and its two
fireplaces... but with a few surprises in store.

The first surprise is the bar counter, a unique triangular brick-built affair that juts out like the
bows of a ship and serves both the public bar and the dining room. The second surprise is the

beer: there's no regular bitter, but a choice of three ever-changing ales mainly from the region's microbreweries such as Grainstore, Barnwell, Milton, and Nethergate. Weston's Old Rosie scrumpy cider is a permanent feature, with Weston's Perry in summer.

The next surprise is the menu. There are an awful lot of American servicemen based in these parts: the old photos of paddle-steamers, streetcars, and jazz greats such as Duke Ellington and Count Basie are all gifts from various members of the US Air Force. And so the Fox's menu has been designed with them in mind: alongside traditional British dishes such as braised lamb shank you'll find American favourites including faji-tas and jambalaya and also chimmy changas – deep-fried double tortillas. All cooked for knowledgeable and demanding customers, so as authentic as you'll find outside the Big Easy itself.

Conington

White Swan
High Street CB3 8LN
Tel 01954 267251

Conington has an enlight-
ened Victorian squire to
thank for its big, spacious,
cheerful village pub. An
alehouse called the Swan
was recorded as far back as
1765; but in 1849 or thereabouts the Conington Hall
estate decided its tenants
deserved something better
and built a brand-new version in the "Tudoresque" style then coming into vogue. The ground-plan is the H-shape characteristic of grand Elizabethan houses, with two gabled bays linked by a crosswing on three sides of a little courtyard, all embellished with leaded windows capped by archaic hood-mouldings.

Inside, though, there are no fusty Tudorisms such as fake beams and head-crackingly low ceilings. All is light, bright, airy, and sunny; and although there is indeed a fireplaces – and a cheery one at that – it has no hint of the inglenook about it. There's also an even lighter, brighter, airier and sunnier conservatory-style dining room looking out over woods and fields. The garden, too, is worthy of note: it's huge, beautifully-maintained, and has one of the best-equipped children's play areas of any pub garden in the county.

The White Swan is very conscious of its history: careful detective work established the age of the present building, and there's a list on show in the bar of all the landlords and ladies since 1765. The present incumbent, Sarah Bleet, is actually the great-great-great-granddaughter of Arthur Lil-ley, licensee from 1885-98. The pub was sold by the Conington Hall estate in the 1930s to a small local brewer, which, through a series of takeovers, eventually became part of the mighty Greene King empire.

Eltisley

The Eltisley
The Green PE19 6TG
Tel 01480 881308
www.theeltisley.com

Formerly the Leeds Arms after the Leeds family of nearby Croxton Park, the Eltisley has recently been reinvented as a very smart, very modern dining pub. The connection with Croxton Park hasn't been forgotten, though: all the pub's organic meat and game comes from the estate and is butchered on the premises.

AT A GLANCE
Opening times: 12-3, 6-11 Tues-Sat; 12-3 Sun Closed Sun evenings and Mon. Food service: 12-2, 6-9.30 Tues-Sat; 12-3 Sun. Mains £9.95-£21. Bar menu. Live jazz first Sun of every month. Wifi/internet access. 6 letting rooms – £35 single, £60 double. Big car park. Patio and garden. **Wheelchair access/disabled toilet and parking bays**. Children welcome; dogs allowed in bar.

And despite the striking new décor – all battleship grey, or perhaps Farrow & Ball grey, both inside and out – the pub hasn't entirely forgotten its roots either. It dates back to at least 1829 and the low ceilings, exposed beams, stone-flagged floors and open fires are still on parade; and although the accent is on food – everything is made on the premises, right down to the bread and the ice-cream – villagers are still welcome to pop in for a pint or two of cask beer from the Charles Wells range, and they are still welcome to bring their dogs with them.

The pub is sort of open-plan, but it's such a warren of bits and pieces that you can always find somewhere private and tucked away to sit, such as the little cosy snug with its wicker chairs down a few steps off the main bar. Of the two dining rooms one is small and intimate, the second larger and grander. Both are elegant backdrops for the Eltisley's superior food.

Fenstanton

King William IV
High St PE28 9JF Tel 01480 462467

The smallest of Fenstanton's three pubs is also its best-known, with a long-established reputation for fine food that spreads far beyond the village itself – which accounts, perhaps, for the size of the pub's car park!

From the outside, the pub scarcely looks big enough to justify such a large car park. It was created from a row of three cottages (the white-painted half-timbered pair being 17th century, the square red-brick one a good deal younger) probably between 1830 and

1837, those being the regnal dates of the eponymous king. The Beer Act, passed in the first year of his reign, sought to tackle a resurgent epidemic of gin-drinking by allowing any reputable householder, on payment of £2, to sell beer and cider. Thousands upon thousands of householders did just that, and many of them named their establishments after their gracious sovereign as a mark of thanks.

Inside, though, it's a different story. Even a fairly humble cottage knocked into one big room makes a fair-sized bar; three of them makes two beamed low-ceilinged bars divided by an enormous brick fireplace; a cosy little snug; and a smart dining room extended by an equally smart conservatory. The décor is comfortable rather than all bare board and brick, with leather sofas in the snug and middle bar; real ales are from Greene King.

Gamlingay

Cock
Church St SG19 3JH
Tel 01767 650255

 At the very heart of Gamlingay, both geographically and socially, the Cock has been quenching local thirsts since at least 1588. It's unusual to have such an early date so well substantiated, and it has been suggested that it was an inn as early as 1435; but 1588 was the year that John Russell, a landlord of the Cock who had earlier been convicted of fornication and slander, died.

Manners here have improved somewhat since then, you'll be glad to hear, and the Cock today is a genuinely welcoming and friendly pub whose warm heart is aptly symbolised by the enormous inglenook fireplace that dominates the lounge bar. (And even that slanderous fornicator John Russell, as it turns out, wasn't as bad as his record suggests: not only did he leave money to charity, he also commissioned the surely unique plaster tablet on the gable end depicting "convivial emblems" including flask, glass, pipe, and corkscrew).

It's a rambling old jigsaw of a place, the Cock. The front rooms have been tentatively dated to the 1560s, and the alarmingly sloping ceiling in the public bar (within living memory let separately as a tailor's shop) is testament to its age. But the roof dates to the late 17th or early 18th century, as does the scalloped ornamentation on the façade; the three dormers with their carved lion's heads are thought to be 19th century; and the dining room at the back was added as a clubroom probably in about 1900 or slightly before. The forest of beams in the lounge bar should give clues to the original layout but are such a jumble that one wonders how many of them are actually in their

original positions. A blocked-up door behind the public bar appears to lead nowhere; there's a mysterious ivy-covered chimney stack at the back which seems never to have had a fireplace; and above the front door is a tiny window lighting an equally tiny room which has been bricked up for longer than anyone can remember.

Originally a farm, the Cock has lost all its outbuildings but has managed to retain a large part of its long, narrow, medieval burgage plot. That means there's plenty of room for a charming patio with comfortable smoking shelter, ample parking, and a big garden with picnic sets, petanque court, and well-equipped children's play area that fills to bursting with family parties whenever the sun deigns to shine.

Every village deserves a pub as well-found, as all-embracing, and indeed as well-run as the Cock, and it's a great pity that so many villages don't have one. Its philosophy, which should perhaps be the philosophy of all pubs, is to provide something for everyone – an ambition in which it succeeds admirably.

The only people not wanted here, in fact, are slanderers and fornicators. Well, slanderers.

Godmanchester

Exhibition
London Road PE29 2HZ Tel 01480 459134

Boy, is this ever a weird place.
From the outside, it's a straightforward little double-fronted red brick cottage with a vaguely Georgian look about it. Its very name dates its conversion to a pub – 1851, the Great Exhibition, right? Nothing special about that – plenty of private houses started retailing beer during the 1830-1869 currency of the Beer Act and later became full-blown pubs. So, nothing exceptional so far.

Then you go inside, and your mind is blown.

Your first impression of the bar is Pizza Express chic – stone-flagged floor, cream walls, no clutter, and a sort of 1980s Peter Mayle Year in Provence cool. Then you clock the trompe l'oiel bookcases that line one wall, and the fake shop-fronts that line the other; and you think: this place was designed by a madman. An imaginative madman, but a madman nonetheless.

The dining room is more sane: the same Mediterranean guiding spirit has inspired the décor, but there are no dummy shopfronts or stunted-up bookshelves to confuse the issue. The stone-flagged floors, the pale beech tables and chairs, the uncluttered cool cream walls – this is the holidays-remembered vibe that is proving more successful than the black-beam olde-worlde approach at tempting many Brits out of their homes of an evening, especially a summer's evening, by evoking the magic of August in Puerto Banus or the South of France.

Mind you, you don't get Greene King IPA or Fuller's London Pride in Puerto Banus. You do here.

AT A GLANCE
Opening times: 11.30-12 all week. Food service: 12-2.30, 6.30-9 Mon-Sat; 12-3, 6.30-8.15 Sun. Sandwiches, etc £3.95-£7.20; mains £4.95-£12.95. Big car park. Well-manicured and obviously loved garden. Children and dogs allowed.

Great Staughton

White Hart
High St PE19 5DA
Tel 01480 860354

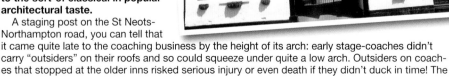

A peach of a pub in a peach of a village, the White Hart hides its 17th-century origins behind a vaguely Georgian front – well, at least, it was given sash windows when the frankly rustic gave way to the sort-of classical in popular architectural taste.

A staging post on the St Neots-Northampton road, you can tell that it came quite late to the coaching business by the height of its arch: early stage-coaches didn't carry "outsiders" on their roofs and so could squeeze under quite a low arch. Outsiders on coaches that stopped at the older inns risked serious injury or even death if they didn't duck in time! The

White Hart has a tall enough arch to accommodate even the tallest outsider. Judging by its size, though, it was never a major stage, but was more likely a post-ing house that made its living mostly from private carriages and post-chases rather than mail-coaches and scheduled public services.

AT A GLANCE
Opening times: 12-2.30, 5-11 Mon-Yhurs; 12-2.30, 5-12 Fri; 12-2.30 6-12 Sat; 12-9.30 Sun. Food service: 12-2, 6.30-8.30 Tues-Sat. Sunday lunch must be booked. Sand-wiches etc around £5. Mains all under £7. Car park. Patio. Garden.

Today, it makes a very cosy village local, comfortable and matter-of-fact and not making too much of a song and dance about its great age despite the regulation low ceilings, black oak beams, and big inglenook fireplace. As well as the bar there's a big games room with a rare Northamptonshire skittles table and a smaller meeting and functions room.

It's one of three pubs in the county owned by Lincolnshire brewer Bate-man's, but as well as Bateman's XB it stocks one or two guest ales from other breweries.

Hartford

King of the Belgians
27 Main St PE29 1XU
Tel 01480 452030

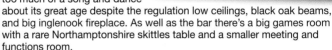

The creation of the Huntingdon ring-road has, as so often hap-pens, left this remarkable little pub completely stranded as far as passing trade is concerned. And yet there's a dividend; for Main Street was once, as its name suggests, the bustling main road to Ramsey and beyond, and what the King of the Belgians has lost in passing trade it has gained in tranquillity.

Hartford has, in recent decades, somewhat lost its identity as a sepa-rate village and become a sprawl-ing suburb of Huntingdon; but this quarter retains something of its old self, and the King of the Belgians still has a core of regulars who can remember it as it was when donkey-races were run past its front door.

The pub claims a date of 1541, and it certainly looks it. The oldest part of the long, low building – there can scarcely be room to stand upright on its upper floor, even for a person of only moder-ate height – has its low ceilings, its blackened oak beams, and its fireplace at either end (one of which still displays what looks suspiciously like a bread-oven). But it has only been recorded as a pub since 1771, which was when Frederick the Great of Prussia was cheering British hearts with a

AT A GLANCE

Opening times:
11-3, 5-11 Mon-Thurs; 11-12
Fri-Sat; 12-11
Sun. Food service:
11.30-2.30 Mon;
11.30-2.30,
5.30-9.30 Tues-Sat; 12-4 Sun.
Sandwiches etc
£3.50-£4.95; mains
£5.95-£9.95. Real
ales: Woodforde's
Wherry, Adnams
Bitter, Courage
Directors. Tiny car
park. Charming
garden with smoking shelter. Children
allowed in dining
room; dogs allowed

run of closely-fought victories against our traditional enemies, the French. Hence the pub's original name, the King of the Prussians. Scroll down 150-odd years and Prussian victories weren't quite so popular; the pub's present name in memory of the gallant Albert I, who refused to knuckle under whatever the odds.

The same is true of the pub: five years ago there was an application to turn it into a private house, but more than 100 objectors were quickly mobilised, and the proposal was rejected by the council.

What the locals' prompt action saved was a long, low, narrow pub with a comfortable and cosy bar that manages to be sunny and bright despite its great age and low ceilings, and a stylish and much more modern dining room that wears its forest of fake beams with great chutzpah.

Hemingford Abbotts

Axe & Compass
High St PE28 9AH
Tel 01480 463605
www.axeandcompass.
co.uk

Seemingly more thatch than wall, the Axe & Compass stands plumb in the middle of the affluent village of Hemingford Abbotts as it has done for maybe 500 years. Its very name betrays its antiquity, for it was originally the Foresters Arms, and there hasn't been much in the way of forestry around here for many a long age. Later – when all the trees had been cut down, presumably – it was the Carpenters Arms. Today its sign unites the tools of both trades.

A very cheerful and bustling local, the Axe & Compass has a comfortable and well-worn public bar with scuffed parquet floors, a little brick fireplace, and low ceilings criss-crossed by beams

AT A GLANCE

Opening times: 12-11 Mon-Fri; 10-11 Sat; 10-10.30 Sun. Food service: 12-2.30, 6-9 Mon-Fri; 12-3, 6-9 Sat; 12-3 Sun. Snacks £3.50-£6.95. Mains £6.95-£10.95. Children's menu. Real ales: Greene King IPA, Black Sheep Bitter, guest. Pool. Games night (pool, darts, skittles) Sun. Car park. Big garden with play equipment. Children and dogs welcome. **Wheelchair access/disabled toilet**.

some of which may even be genuine – especially in the lounge bar at the side, which looks like the oldest part of the building. The newest part is undoubtedly the long, narrow dining room with its polished wooden floors and big French windows; and in fact you can see in the lounge pictures from the 1930s that show the old outbuildings being brought into use and the original tiny windows being replaced with much bigger ones.

A great place for beer, food, and entertainment, the Axe & Compass is the epitome of a pub that provides something for everyone and proves that, well-run and without too heavy a burden of rent, village pubs are still viable and valued.

Hemingford Grey

Cock
47 High St PE28 9BJ
Tel 01480 463609
www.cambscuisine.com

Given that it's owned by celebrated restaurateur Oliver Thain of the Boathouse, Ely, and the Cambridge Chop House, and given also the well-heeled demographic of Hemingford Grey, the Cock is understandably best known for its food.

And it's true the food is serious here: with mains ranging from £12-£17 and sandwiches at £7, you've got to take it seriously. The dining room is a serious place, too: clean and cool, full of light and air, with muted pale peach and eau-de-nil walls and highly polished floorboards, it has a calm, quiet atmosphere – not quite a temple of gastronomy; more a library. You'd certainly feel self-conscious if you laughed too loudly here.

But the Cock isn't just a restaurant. The bar remains stubbornly pubby. The décor, true, is just as clean and contemporary (no horsebrasses, and the beams are painted that Farrow & Ball-style putty colour which actually looks far nicer than it sounds); but it's less posh and certainly lest

Opening times:
11.30-3, 6-11
Mon-Sat; 12-4,
6.30-10.30 Sun.
Food service:
12-2.30, 6.30-9
Mon-Thurs (9.30
Fri-Sat); 12-2.30,
6.30-8.30 Sun.
Car park. Smok-
ing shelter. Big
and very beautiful
garden. Chil-
dren allowed in
restaurant. Dogs
allowed in bar.

sedate than the dining room. You can't eat in the bar; and bar and dining room even have separate street doors. There's also evidence in the shape of five hand-pumps that Thain both knows and cares much more than most restaura-teurs about beer. It's no afterthought or sop fas far as he's concerned: he believes that the beers his establishments serve should be of just as fine a quality and just as local as the ingredients used in his kitchens. Hence the presence not only of Buntingford Highwayman IPA (from Hertfordshire), of Wolf Golden Jackal (from Norfolk), and of two guest ales from other micro-brewers of the region, but also of Cromwell Cider, from this very village.

Holywell

Old Ferry Boat
PE27 4TG
Tel 01480 498012
www.oldferryboat.com

 The Old Ferry Boat is one of the half-dozen or so top contenders for the most ludi-crously bogus yet hotly-contested accolade in Britain, that of "England's oldest inn", claiming an utterly unsupported and indeed impossible to substantiate date of origin of 560.

Archaeologists, it is true, have found traces of occupancy on the site from the late 5th century; but it's a long way from finding a few courses of masonry to establishing the presence of a pub. On top of that, there are only a handful of identifi-ably Saxon buildings in the whole country; commercial inns (as opposed to monastic hospices) and urban taverns only began to emerge in the 13th century; and country alehouses can only be proven from the late 14th. So: 560? 1560, more like!

(The story of Juliet Tewsley, the 17-year-

old girl buried under stone slab in the bar having committed suicide after being jilted by the local woodcutter, is also the stuff of ballad rather than fact; and even if there is a true story lurking there, it certainly doesn't go back to the 11th century when the forename Juliet was unknown and only the aristocracy had surnames).

Nevertheless, and historical debunking apart, the oldest part of the building, the range fronting the river, is undeniably ancient and feels it, despite several rebuildings and a series of extensions over the years.

If there were a competition for best-located inn, though, the Old Ferry Boat would definitely be in with a shout, set as it is on a tranquil stretch of the Great Ouse. Even on a dank and drizzly day you can tell how popular it is and how busy it can get from the size of the car park and the number of tables on the riverside terrace – 42, to be precise, so the garden seats almost as many people as the pub itself does!

And make no mistake, the Old Ferry Boat is a big, big, pub, all tricked out inside in brewer's best mock-Tudor but saved from being cavernous by numerous partitions of fake studwork and other such devices. The genuinely old part is easy to tell from the modern pastiche; but the pastiche isn't bad – certainly much, much better than similar efforts of the 1970s and '80s.

Huntingdon

George Hotel
George St PE27 3AB
Tel 01480 432444

 Huntingdon's main thoroughfare, before the town was by-passed, was Ermine Street, also known as the Old North Road; and with its medieval bridge over the Ouse, the town has always been strategically important. No surprise, then, that its principal (and last surviving) inn, the George, has been a well-known stopover on the London-Edinburgh road since at least 1510.

It's also one of the few old inns that can genuinely boast both Oliver Cromwell and Charles I as guests. It came into the possession of the Cromwell family in about 1550: Old Noll's dad is buried in the churchyard next door and the Lord Protector himself went to school just across the road. And when the royalists briefly captured the town in 1645, Charles I chose the George as his HQ.

The inn that Charles and his nemesis knew has gone almost without trace, although they might still recognise the two original timber-framed 17th-century sides of the yard, one of them still possessing its open gallery and coach entrance with carved pillars; the other, perhaps a little older, having a jettied upper floor and an external staircase. These are, unfortunately, the only survivors of a disastrous fire in 1870 which utterly destroyed the inn itself and the other two sides of what had been the biggest inn-yard in the country (in its heyday the George was a coaching inn of the first rank, rehorsing and victualling a dozen scheduled London-York services a day as well as local traffic): the destroyed portions, it has to be said, were rather plainly replaced.

For although the hotel is fine enough in its Victorian way – and it's certainly very smart and very civilised – it's the yard that people come to see, especially in late June and early July, when it is transformed into an extremely professional-looking outdoor auditorium for Shakespeare at the George. This year's performance, The Taming of the Shrew, marks the 50th anniversary of Shakespeare at the George; and indeed it was the first production back in 1959 and was also performed for the 21st anniversary in 1980.

Market Inn
Raitts Passage, Market Hill PE29 3NG
Tel 01480 453332

The Market Inn claims to be Tudor in origin, although it's been restored, refurbished, and altered so many times over the years that it looks today more like Brewers' Tudor. The stained-glass panels in its windows saying "Tap Room", "Saloon Bar", "Smoke Room" and "Parlour" are probably about a century old, as is the appliqué timber framing on the frontage.

It is thought to have originally been a row of cottages belonging to the old Fountain Hotel on Market Hill, and how long it has been a pub nobody seems quite certain. One thing you can be sure of is that it hasn't been here, peeking coyly out of its little side-street, for quite as many centuries as the market it used to serve – that was chartered in 1252!

However historical or otherwise the building itself might be, though, it is the direct descendant of the very first pubs in England. When Huntingdon market was chartered, brewers only sold ale to take away. People didn't drink in pubs, because there weren't any. They brought their ale by the gallon or half-gallon (a "pottle") and drank it at home. But on market days, when peasants would pour in from the surrounding countryside to buy and sell, brewers started setting up stalls of their own – so-called "tabernae", which is Latin for booths – where shoppers and other stallholders could buy ale by the pint to drink on the spot. This habit of sociable drinking on market days, which many peasants regarded as holidays, caught on; and in time brewers began inviting drinkers into their own kitchens on a regular basis, thus creating the forerunners of today's pub.

AT A GLANCE
Opening times: 11-11.30 Mon-Sat; 11-11 Sun. Hot snacks all day 95p-£1.25. Karaoke Mon; live bands Sat; regular quizzes; pool; darts; big-screen TV (terrestrial only). Smokers' shelter. Dogs welcome; children not.

You might not feel especially medieval as you sup your pint (Young's Bitter, Potbelly Beijing Black, plus changing guest) in the cosy surroundings of the Market Inn, where there is neither spit nor sawdust but instead a big comfortable open-plan bar with a lounge area and a separate games room. But the bustle, the pub games, the live music, and the hot snacks are all features, mutatis mutandis, that a late medieval drinker would still recognise and appreciate.

Keyston

Pheasant
Village Loop PE28 0RE
Tel 01823 710241
www.thepheasant-keyston.co.uk

The Pheasant has long had a reputation as one of the finest dining pubs in West Cambridgeshire; but even if all it served was egg and chips it would still be worth a visit.

For the Pheasant is as pretty as a picture: a long, low, whitewashed affair under a beetling thatched roof, originally a row of 16th-century cottages but trading as a pub under the name the White Swan since at least 1908. When you arrive, you think that this must surely epitomise the traditional village   pub; and then you go inside and see what they've done with tradition. They've turned it on its head is what they've done.

All the elements are still in place: the great big fireplace, the cream-painted walls, the absolute forest of oak beams. Well, almost all the elements are in place. One that isn't is the low ceiling. In fact there's no ceiling at all in the bar, which is open all the way up to the roof – all the way being,

in this case, not very far. You wonder how anyone could have stood upright at all when the first floor had a floor. The space, as well as the complete absence of rusti-cana, makes the genuinely ancient bits and pieces feel almost modern, an illusion heightened by the smart leather-upholstered restaurant chairs and the sofas and armchairs that go with them.

If all this says gastropub – as might the French-inspired menus, the three separate dining rooms, and the facts that proprietors Jay and Taffeta Scrimshaw both come from the restaurant world, own their own herd of cattle and flock of sheep, and have rare-breed pigs raised exclusively for them – be consoled by the beers. Up to four of them come from local brewers such as Grainstore, Buntingford, Potbelly and Barnwell, and they change all the time.

Kimbolton

New Sun
20 High St PE28 0HA
Tel 01480 860052

Kimbolton is, let's face it, dead posh. Halfway between large village and small town, it's stuffed with beautiful Georgian (and older) houses, has an air of the Cotswolds about it, and has an ex-stately home in the middle which is now a well-known public school. So even if the inhabitants of Kimbolton weren't posh, the mums and dads purring up in the Roller every few weekends to take their sprog and chums out for a spot of lunch would make it posh.

And therefore the New Sun is posh. Behind the Georgian

façade lurks a much, much older building – something you realise the moment you step through the front door into the lounge and spot the exposed timbers of the building's 16th-century frame.

AT A GLANCE
Opening times: 11.30-2.30, 6-11 Mon-Sat; 12-10.30 Sun. Cask ales: Charles Wells Eagle and Bombardier plus guest. Food service: 12-2.15, 7-9.30 Mon-Sat; 12-2.30 Sun. Tapas etc £1.20-£5.95. À la carte mains £10.25-£22. No car park. Garden. Heated and covered patio. Children welcome. Dogs allowed in bar and lounge.

But it doesn't play on its antiquity: the accent is on a restrained good taste more in tune with the Georgian façade than the Tudor carcase. The sofa is tasteful; the armchairs are tasteful; the prints are tasteful; the mirror is tasteful. Even the lighting is tasteful. The good taste continues right through the bar to the conservatory-style restaurant at the back (one of two) which, with its tiled floor, French windows and big skylight, has more of a Mediterranean vibe than a Georgian-England one. But it's still tasteful.

Which makes it all the more amazing that the favourite form of entertainment hereabouts is to have impressionists or rather "tribute artists" – Freddie Mercury, Tom Jones, Rod Stewart and, of course, Elvis – strolling through the bar and restaurants serenading diners and drinkers at their tables. It somehow restores one's faith in human nature to find that posh, tasteful people are as bonkers as the rest of us really.

Leighton Bromswold

Green Man
37 The Avenue PE28 5AW Tel 01480 890238

As cheery a village local as you could wish to find, the Green Man is a near-perfect stereotype of the olde-worlde English country pub.

In the bar there are faded carpets, scrubbed tables, low ceilings, black oak beams, horse-brasses by the yard, high-backed settles and, of course, an inglenook fireplace. The dining room is slightly more gentrified and utterly charming. The cask beers, four of them, are all from local independent breweries and change constantly. The food is well-priced and substantial and the entertainments include darts, pool, dominoes, crib and – possibly the noisiest of pub games – Northamptonshire skittles.

The place has history, too, lots of it; you can tell that just by looking. But the shape of its history is vague enough to be a source of agreeable dispute. The orthodox version is that it was originally a row of cottages, possibly rooted in the Middle Ages, that were later knocked together to become a coaching inn. And it certainly has adequate outbuildings for the job. The only problem with this thesis is that a coaching inn requires a coaching road; and although the street on which the pub stands has wide enough verges to have once been a drove, it doesn't actually go from anywhere to anywhere, and apparently never did.

More likely, I think, is that it was originally a substantial farm (and they do say it used to have paddocks) that brewed beer for its own labourers and progressed to brewing beer for sale. It certainly wouldn't be the only one.

Little Gransden

Chequers
71 Main Rd SG19
3DW
Tel 01767 677348

To be brutally honest, the Chequers doesn't look much from the outside. A long, plain building of the locally ubiquitous Cambridgeshire grey brick, it was built about 1900 to replace a much older thatched red-brick pub – probably early 18th century, but recorded as licensed only from 1817 – after a disastrous fire.

But if it's no oil painting, it's still one of Cambridgeshire's truly great country pubs. Leased (and later bought outright) from Whitbread by Sid Mitchell in 1951 after his demob from the RAF, the pub is still run by his son Bob and daughter-in-law Wendy. Bob knows everybody, has time for everybody, and never forgets a face. When he's not at work in the Son of Sid Brewery – you can watch him at it through the lounge bar window – Bob holds court in the tiny lobby-like middle bar, which despite having room for just two stools, two benches, and a small table, is heated to toasting point by an unusually efficient open fire. Plainly decorated with brown-painted pine dadoes, a quarry-tiled floor and swags of dried hops over the bar, it's a great meeting place for villagers; but it also attracts drinkers from a wide surrounding area – all of whom Bob seems to recognise and know by name.

The lounge contains almost the only surviving part of the original Chequers. The fire destroyed it right down to a few courses of brick and a single gable end; but the floor of the lounge and the cellars below belong to the earlier pub. There's an incredibly popular folk night here on the first Thursday of every month, when musicians gather from literally miles around. The pub's third room, at the far end of the building, is home to the TV and pool table and gives the younger (and less folk music-friendly) inhabitants of the village something to do.

Longstowe

Red House
134 Old North Rd
CB3 7UT
Tel 01954 718480
www.theredhouse
-pub.co.uk

A lonely house of welcome on an otherwise deserted stretch of the Old North Road, the Red House was once a busy posting house known as the Golden Lion. Originally it stood on a crossroads, so as well as north-south traffic on the Old North Road itself there was also trade from the Porters Way between Cambridge and Biggleswade until it was closed in the 1860s to make way for the Bedford to Cambridge railway line. The old road is now a bridleway, and is one of several good, long, appetite-sharpening walks in the area.

The Golden Lion wasn't first recorded as an inn until 1800, but there's evidence of a much older building behind the red brick façade with its Strawberry Hill Gothic first-floor windows: the façade and the interior are actually of different heights, so the window openings don't quite match the ceiling joists. It's thought there was a much earlier farm on the site, and when it was turned into an inn the owner of Longstowe Hall imposed a covenant giving him the right to all the manure from the new stables, which could accommodate 39 horses. In fact it was even called the New Stables Inn in the mid-19th century before adopting its present name.

The Red House's rather isolated position makes the bar seem even cosier and more welcoming. It's fairly plain and unfussy, with a big brick fireplace and scrubbed pine tables, an understated smidgeon of rusticana, and murals by a local artist. Down a few steps at the back there's a comfortable lounge with armchairs and sofas on a quarry-tiled floor; and off to one side there's a surprisingly big,

bright, airy dining-room with more quarry-tiles on the floor and even a piano whose ivories occasionally get tickled. Alongside the four ever-changing real ales is traditional cider from Cam Valley, one of several new farm cidermakers springing up in the county.

Offord Darcy

Horseshoe
PE15 5RH
Tel 01480 810293
www.thehorseshoeinn.biz

It can be a disheartening time for many pubgoers when their local is taken over by a chef. Will the crisp white tablecloths, more knives and forks than seem possible, monstrous wine-lists, and crab cakes with lime, chilli, and ginger dressing leave any room for the humble pint-and-a-pork-pie people?

At the venerable Horseshoe in the straggling village of Offord Darcy, the answer was

yes. Richard Kennedy, who took over in 2007, is indeed a chef whose cv includes spells at some of Cambridgeshire's top restaurants; but his roots are in the pub trade. As a teenager in Northill, Bedfordshire, his best friends ran the Crown. "My first job was in the kitchen at the Crown," he says. "I pulled my first pint at the Crown. The first time I passed out was in the Crown – and the first pub I got thrown out of was the Crown!"

Other than brightening up the place by dumping the burgundy upholstery and curtains and replacing worn-out parquet with pale oak floorboards, Richard hasn't had to change much. But it's still quite a shock when you walk into the main bar: the pub claims a date of origin of 1626, so you might well expect to find horse-brasses, black oak beams, and an inglenook full of labradors. What you get is light, space, and air. The snug, home of the widescreen TV and fruit machines, is more pubby, but still not exactly olde-worlde.

And in the space he's created, Richard has consciously tried to establish a balance between drinkers and diners. For the drinkers, there's Potton Brewery's

Shannon IPA, Fuller's London Pride, and two changing guests, often including Ossian Ale from Inveralmond of Perth. (The family used to live near the brewery). There's bar food, too: sandwiches and baguettes, soup and a roll at £4, fish and chips at £8, a Sunday carvery at £10. The restaurant menu is a bit more elevated: whole sea-bream with citrus quinoa, garlic and rosemary roast pheasant with smoked bacon mash, and breast of barbary duck with sour cherry and pear balsamic reduction aren't standard pub fare. The important thing for Richard is making sure that pint-swillers and fine diners alike can feel the Horseshoe is theirs.

"We've got millionaires who think nothing of fillet steak and Margaux at £50 a head, and retired farmworkers who come in every day but only have a pint," he says. "What we like is that they all sit next to each other and get on. That's what creates the atmosphere."

Old Weston

Swan
Main St PE28 5LL
Tel 01832 293400

Two 16th-century cottages knocked into one, the Old Swan was a recorded as a smithy in the 1841 census and might therefore be a "Beer Act" alehouse – that is, one that came into being during the 40-year currency of the 1830 Beer Act that allowed any householder to retail beer on payment of a two-guinea fee. In earlier centuries blacksmiths had generally offered a mug of home-brew to customers whose horses were being

shod, and many progressed from there to full-time alehouse-keeper. Perhaps the smith of the 1841 census was taking advantage of the Beer Act to revive an old tradition?

At any rate, the Old Swan has served ale to the villagers since then; and its low-ceilinged bar has at its heart a big brick fireplace as cheerful as any blacksmith's forge. It also offers the traditional entertainment of Northamptonshire or "hood" skittles and has a team in a local league. Sadly, though, the villagers no longer seem to want a lunchtime pint on weekdays, so from Monday to Friday the Old Swan only opens in the evenings.

Pidley

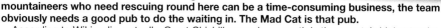

Mad Cat
High St PE28 3BX
Tel 01487 842245
www.madcatinn.co.uk

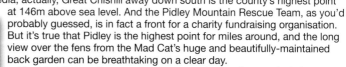

Claiming, as it does, to be the highest village in Cambridgeshire, Pidley obviously needs a mountain rescue team. And as waiting for mountaineers who need rescuing round here can be a time-consuming business, the team obviously needs a good pub to do the waiting in. The Mad Cat is that pub.

According to Wikipedia, actually, Great Chishill away down south is the county's highest point at 146m above sea level. And the Pidley Mountain Rescue Team, as you'd probably guessed, is in fact a front for a charity fundraising organisation. But it's true that Pidley is the highest point for miles around, and the long view over the fens from the Mad Cat's huge and beautifully-maintained back garden can be breathtaking on a clear day.

The Mad Cat, so they say, has been perched up here on its lofty eminence since the early 17th century. For most of that time it was the White Lion; crude signpainting and a lively sense of humour gave it its present name about a century ago. A popular food pub, it has a big and very smart dining room boasting a huge fireplace with an elaborate Edwardian overmantel and an aquarium of almost equal size. Recalling Oliver Goldsmith's description of an inn-kitchen ornamented with "broken teacups, wisely kept for show", the big rafter in the middle of the ceiling is hung with (unbroken) china plates and jugs. Hunting prints on the walls mark the pub's popularity with the local shooting fraternity.

And although it's well-regarded as a food pub, beer is not neglected at the Mad Cat. The bar is small but bright and sunny, and the quality of its constantly changing line-up of real ales from local brewers such as Elgood's and Oakham has won it the 2009 Pub of the Year award from the local branch of the Campaign for Real Ale.

Floods Tavern
27 The Broadway PE27 4TG
Tel 01480 467773
www.floods-tavern.com

George Yard, Unicorn House, Cow & Hare Passage – The Broadway is strewn with memorials to the coaching inns, posthouses and pubs that lined it in the 18th and 19th centuries. Now all that's left is Floods Tavern, which is also 18th century but was actually a bank when The Broadway's inns were flourishing and has only been licensed since 1977. The name is a literal description of what happens to the back garden – and sometimes to the pub itself – whenever the Great Ouse rises too far.

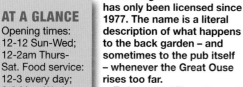

AT A GLANCE
Opening times: 12-12 Sun-Wed; 12-2am Thurs-Sat. Food service: 12-3 every day; 6-9 Mon-Wed. Lght lunches £1.75-£4.95; mains £5.25-£6.95; children's menu £3.50. Wifi/internet access. South-facing riverside terrace. Children and dogs welcome.

Today one of Elgood's most southerly outposts, Floods is a cheerful, buzzy town-centre local with two bars and a dining room whose decorative scheme of patterned carpets, bare brick, mulberry paint, and black beams (some of them genuine!) seems more accidental than planned, and is none the worse for that. The beer is excellent, the food is well-priced, and the pub is also a centre for entertainment in St Ives, with satellite sports on three big screens, bar billiards, karaoke on Thursdays and live bands in the dining-room – they clear away the tables, so diners don't have to compete with the band's PA system – on Fridays and Saturdays.

Oliver Cromwell
13 Wellington St PE27 5AZ Tel 01480 465601 www.theolivercromwell.com

They probably don't hold much with decapitating monarchs in St Ives these days – their MP is, after all, John Major, who is not a noted republican – but like Huntingdon and Ely, they're still fiercely proud of their links with the district's most famous son and you find the Lord Protector celebrated almost everywhere.

In the case of the Oliver Cromwell, though, there is a genuine background of radical politics. It was first recorded as a beer-house called the Feathers in the 1840s, a decade of revolutionary upheavals throughout Europe. The owner, Henry How, who later retired to a toll house which he renamed Republic Cottage, changed the pub's name and also founded a brewery there. His son Arthur, also known as a republican, expanded the brewery and took over the wine and spirits licence and the wrought iron sign bracket from the Ship further up the street (now the Riverside Restaurant).

Brewing stopped at the Oliver Cromwell in 1919 when the third generation of the How family sold up, and it withdrew from its role as a hotbed of subversion to become one of the prettiest pubs in St Ives, as well as one its best ale-houses. On offer in the big pine-panelled bar are Adnams Bitter, Woodforde's Wherry, Oakham JHB and up to three guests, as well as farmhouse cider from Cromwell (that name again!) of Hemingford Abbots. At the back of the pub is a smart, sunny dining room with stripped floorboards, a pine dado, highly-polished tables, and the old well that used to supply the brewery.

AT A GLANCE

Opening times: 11-11 Mon-Wed; 11-11.30 Thurs; 11-12.30 Fri-Sat; 12-11 Sun. Food service: 12-2.45 Mon-Sat. Sandwiches etc £3.75-£6.20; specials/mains £4.95-£10.95. Live music 9-11 Thurs. Heated patio and covered courtyard. Children and dogs welcome.

White Hart
Sheep Market PE27 5AH
Tel 01480 463275

A record of a fire breaking out in White Hart Lane in 1689 tells us that this is the oldest surviving pub in St Ives. It is also one of only two inns named on a list compiled in the 1730s that still trades – and as the other, the Dolphin, was demolished and rebuilt as a severely modern hotel in the 1980s, the accolade of oldest pub definitely goes to the White Hart.

One of three pubs fronting the town's market place (where once there were 19!), the White Hart is an early 18th-century coaching house – it was the base for a regular coach service to Cam-

AT A GLANCE

Opening times:
10-30-11.30 Mon-
Thurs; 10.3-12.30
Fri-Sat; 12-10.30
Sun. Food serv-
ice: 12-2.30, 7-9
Tues-Fri; 12-3,
7-9 Sat; 12-3
Sun-Mon. Mains
£5.50-£10.50.
Real ales: Greene
King IPA, Fuller's
London Pride.
4 letting rooms:
£35 single, £50
double. Car park.
Pleasant court-
yard. Children and
dogs welcome.

bridge in the 1830s – whose smartly pan-elled bar with its leather-covered easy chairs retains the civilised ambience of the coffee room of a prosperous Georgian inn.

But the décor here is in fact a compara-tively recent reconstruction: within living memory the present bar was let out as a barber's shop, and the snug across the hallway was the hotel bar – the letter-box in the snug's door is the giveaway, and also indicates that the stone-flagged hallway was probably once an alley.

St Neots

Chequers
St Mary's Street,
Eynesbury
PE19 2TA
Tel 01480
472116

Plenty of pubs claim to be haunt-ed, but their ghost stories are usually just that – stories. Somebody's great-uncle's brother-in-law, or the last ten-ant but two, is said to have seen the ghost, but that was a few years ago.

Well, Shirley Lamb has actually seen the ghost in her pub. She was bringing fresh flowers into the bar one morning and there he was, sitting in the rocking-chair beside the ancient inglenook fireplace. When she came in he stood up, and seemed to be a tall man of at least 6ft, aged in his 40s and wearing a long black gown. Then he vanished.

Well, it was morning; so spirits of the liquid kind can be ruled out. But whether you see the ghost for yourself or not, you will see plenty of fresh flowers at the Chequers. They are lovely to see, and add a distinguished touch to an already distinguished pub. For if the Chequers is not grand or imposing, it is certainly ancient – ancient enough to have a ghost in a long black gown, in fact. The oldest parts are claimed to be 15th century, and the small bar with its

AT A GLANCE

Opening times: 12-2.30, 6.30-11 Tues-sat; 12-2.30 Sun. Closed Sunday evenings and Mondays. Food service: bar snacks 12-2; dining room open 12-2, 6.45-9 Tues-Sat, 12-2 Sun. Mains £6.95-£19.95. Two courses £9.95, evenings only. Large car park. Delightful secluded garden.

low ceiling and heavy oak beams, its old local photographs and scattering of horse-brasses, lives up to its location in the quaintest part of St Neots.

It's also the town's best dining pub, with a slightly less ancient 50-cover dining room and a well-established reputation for the standard of its cooking. The ale's not bad, either, with a choice of the locally-brewed Golden Newt from Elgood's of Wisbech or Thwaites Bitter from just a bit further afield – Blackburn, Lancashire, to be precise.

Crown

Great North Road, Eaton Socon
PE19 8EN
Tel 01480 212232

With its undulating roof and tiny bay windows, the long, low, 17th-century Crown is about as close as it's possible to get to the ideal vision of the chocolate-box English pub. Shame about the location, then; for what must once have been a pretty little roadside beerhouse (the road in this case being the Great North Road) now finds itself marooned in a wasteland of ring-roads and roundabouts, with a retail park on one side, an office development on the other, and a leisure complex just across the road.

The back's not that pretty, either: they've built a huge Premier Inn there, whose guests have their breakfasts and dinners in the Crown – but as it's their custom that has ensured the Crown's survival, perhaps we shouldn't begrudge them their big mauve motel.

For the Crown itself is spectacularly pretty both outside and in. The bar in older part at the front of the building is exactly as it should be, with loads of genuinely ancient beams and bits of exposed timber studwork to show where the internal partitions once were. There's a single surviving fireplace and lots of odd corners and bays, including a cosy little snug off to one side, to break it all up into more intimate spaces.

The big new dining extension at the back isn't half bad, either: modern designers are much better than their predecessors in the 1970s and '80s at creating olde-worlde pastiches: if the beams here aren't structural, at least they're recovered rather than machine-made; and there are plenty of high-backed settles and other devices to break up what would otherwise be a barn.

The beer's a treat here, too: the Crown is part of a large managed-house pub chain but has turned its back resolutely on mass-produced fizz and started experimenting with cask ales from lesser-known microbrewers. There are up to three at a time on handpump, always changing – and not too cold, either, which is the usual sin of big managed dining pubs. A wide menu includes regular fish specials.

Lord John Russell

25 Russell St PE19 1BA
Tel 01480 406330
www.lordjohnrussell.
co.uk

The Lord John Russell has for a while been the town centre's stand-out alehouse, if for no better reason than that it is one of the three Cambridgeshire pubs that belong to legendary Lincolnshire brewer Bateman's.

Actually, the pub has a lot going against it. It's not especially picturesque or historic (it takes its name from the second son of the Duke of Bedford who was Prime Minister in the 1860s, which dates it pretty neatly); the décor is pleasant enough but very modern and not exactly breathtakingly lovely; and there's no car park and no on-street parking anywhere nearby either (and don't even think of trying to drive down Russell Street!).

But this is not only a well-loved community local of the sort you don't find so frequently nowadays, it's also the pub of choice for the St Neots beer-lover, with not only three ales from Bateman's permanently on tap, but three changing guests as well, two of them served straight from the barrels. There's real Herefordshire cider from Weston's too, and spring and autumn beer festivals that have become landmark events on the town's social calendar.

Not only is the beer good, the food (now served in a brand new and very pleasant dining room) is getting something of a reputation too, especially the steakstones – hot stones brought to your table on which you can cook your steak or fish to your liking. Another new development is the smart little garden, complete with patio heaters and parasols for the protection of smokers, and grassed over with Astroturf.

Millers Arms
38 Ackerman St, Eaton
Socon
PE19 8HR
Tel 01480 405965

That cliched old sign "Duck or Grouse" is such a common sight in low-ceilinged old pubs that people tend not to notice it any more. Big mistake here – even a man of medium height can easily get a nasty scrape from some of the doorways; so if you're not the type who takes any notice of notices, wear a hard hat.

For the Millers Arms is a genuine antique of a pub, probably 16th century, with a spectacularly sloping ceiling in the bar that makes one wonder what the floors upstairs must be like. And, indeed, how tall a man of medium height actually was back then in the 16th century. It has all the accoutrements of age – beams, tiled floors, big fireplace – but it also has a brand new dining room in a big conservatory-style extension at the back

where the steaks are a bit
special in that they don't
come from cows. They
come from ostriches,
kangaroos, impala, rein-
deer; any species, in fact,
that will yield up a good
piece of grilling meat.

As well as its range of
"steaks of the world", the
Miller's Arms is known for
its live music (Wednes-
day and Friday evenings)
and for its sign, which
depicts the old flourmill
on the Great Ouse a few
hundred yards away,
which is now better-
known as the Rivermill
Tavern. The only case
I've ever come across
of a pub advertising its
nearest competitor on
its sign!

Pig 'n' Falcon
New Street
PE19 1AE
Tel 07951 785678
www.pignfalcon.
co.uk

**The Victorian terraces
to the north of St Neots
High Street and Market
Square are developing
quite a collection of de-
cent real ale pubs. The
Olde Sun is the most
picturesque of them;
the Hyde Park under
new management has
splashed out on a new
range of beers; for
the Lord John Russell
see above; and most
recently the Falcon has
joined the circuit with
a bullet.**

As a straightforward
tied tenancy the Falcon
was, to be frank, mori-

bund. A small-ish late Georgian or possibly early Victorian backstreet local, it was trying to compete with the style bars on the high street – Sourz on the Optic, and half the available floor-space taken up by a DJ's console and PA. Nobody came, so the new tenants – father and son team John and Brett Nunn – struck a deal with Greene King that allowed them to buy in cask beers from regional microbreweries; changed the pub's name (slightly); applied a few coats of rather more striking paint; and ripped out the trade kitchen (which hadn't been used for years) to make way for stillage for guest brewers' barrels.

AT A GLANCE
Opening times: 10am-12.30am Mon-Wed; 10am-1.30 Thurs; 10am-2.30am Fri-Sat; 11am-12.30 Sun. Food service: snacks £1-£3. Live bands Mon, Fri, Sat (jazz jam every other Mon); open mic Wed. No car park, but Waitrose car park next door is free after 6pm. Covered and heated patio. Under-16s until 6pm. Dogs welcome.

The pub now has the Greene King range on handpump, and, on stillage, two permanent ales – Potbelly Pigs Do Fly and Oakham Inferno – six guests from microbrewers across the region, and at least two and sometimes four farmhouse ciders. The result has so far been electrifying, with busy sessions where under the previous regime the bar staff had outnumbered the customers. Three cheers to new tenant John Nunn for having the imagination to spot the goldmine hidden under all those layers of neglect, and four cheers to Greene King for having the vision to spot the pub's potential as a virtual free house.

Rivermill Tavern
School Lane, Eaton Socon
PE19 8GW
Tel 01480 219612
www.rivermilltavern.co.uk

Whoever decided that Eaton Socon's old flourmill, a gaunt yellow-brick industrial building dating from 1847, would make a good pub was inspired. Because it really has got everything. The building itself is full of character and history (it was for a long time a repair shop for narrowboats), and heavy-duty industrial-strength oak beams as well. The picturesque setting, beside an old wharf that is now a narrow-boat marina, is idyllic. And the conversion, which goes back to 1985 and includes a big dining room on a mezzanine floor overlooking the bar, was both imaginative and well-executed.

As if that weren't enough, the place is well-run by people who know how to attract a crowd. It's famous for its beers, which

AT A GLANCE
Opening times: 12-11 Sat-Thurs; 12-12 Fr. Food service: 12-2.30, 6.30-9.30 Mon-Fri;12-9.30 Sat-Sun. Wifi/internet access. Small car park. Covered patio; riverside terrace. Children welcome.

are Greene King IPA and Abbot, Adnams Broadside, and two constantly changing guests. The menu is well-priced and wide-ranging, with a "crunch lunch" at £5.95 and mains from £6.75 right up to £15.95. And it's also a very popular music venue, with live bands on Fridays and an open mic night every Tuesday, when local bands can use the house PA and drums to make their public début, get experience of live performance, or try out new numbers.

With a local like this, the flats on the other bank of the marina must be the perfect place to live.

White Horse
Great North Road, Eaton Socon
PE19 8EL
Tel 01480 474453
www.whitehorseinn.co.uk

 The largest of many old coaching inns and posthouses that line the old Great North Road as it wends through Eaton Socon, the brick-fronted and creeper-clad Georgian Old White Horse stands on foundations that go back at least to the 15th century if not further. Refronted as a posthouse in the early 18th century, it did not become a major coaching inn until the large, square north wing was added two or three generations later.

Not only is the Old White Horse old, it has great literary connections as well. Before it was extended, it was the model both for the Black Lion in Tobias Smollett's Sir Launcelot Greaves and for the inn in Goldsmith's The Deserted Village. Smollett describes its kitchen, which we may take to be typical, thus: "The kitchen ... was paved with red bricks, remarkably clean, furnished with three or four Windsor chairs, adorned with shining plates of pewter and copper saucepans nicely scoured; a cheerful fire of sea-coal blazed in the chimney."

Goldsmith takes us to the parlour:

> The whitewashed wall, the nicely sanded floor,
> The varnished clock that clicked behind the door.
> The hearth, except when winter ruled the day,
> With aspen boughs and flowers of fennel gay,
> While broken teacups, wisely kept for show,
> Ranged o'er the chimney, glistened in a row.

In 1838 the inn, extended by now, played host to Dickens, who was travelling north on the Glasgow Mail to research local colour for Nicholas Nickleby and, in particular, Dotheboys Hall. He was so struck with the White Horse that he used it for the scene in which Squeers and his caravan of doomed boys break their northward journey to dine.

The amazing thing about the Old White Horse is that it's one of the very few old coaching inns that still has the feel of one. Along the front is a range of four rooms, two of them tiny, all crowded with beams and little fireplaces and equipped with bays where you could sit and watch out for your coach.

Behind, through an engraved wooden screen whose carving is crude enough to be 17th century, or very early 18th, is a great hall that gives on to a proper old-fashioned hotel dining room. A narrow corridor leads to a smaller private dining and functions room. The old inn yard is now the car park and garden, complete with smoker's shelter, but a red-brick coach-house and a range of stables survive, albeit under different ownership.

Despite its age, its atmosphere of antiquity, and its literary heritage, there's nothing grand or formal about the place, though. The bars are very much locals' bars – they even get to vote on which guest ales will complement the regular line-up of Flowers Original and Fuller's London Pride.

AT A GLANCE

Opening times: 12-3, 5-11 Mon-Thurs; 12-3, 5-11.30 Fri-Sat; 12-3, 5-10.30 Sun. Food service: 12-2.30, 6.30-9.30 Tues-Sat; 12-2.30, 6-8 Mon-Sun. Mains £5.95-£11.95 Two letting rooms: £49 single, £56 double. Children and dogs welcome.

Spaldwick

George
High Street PE28 0TD
Tel 01480 890293
www.georgeofspaldwick.
co.uk

The utterly charming George with its crumpled gable-end may not look much like one, but in the late 17th-century it was the equivalent of a filling station.

The building itself is recorded as a substantial private house as far back as 1584, and in the 1670s it paid the highest hearth-tax in the village. By then it was also a blacksmith's forge, and from 1676 it appears in local records as the George, the path from smithy to alehouse being well-worn.

The High Street that passes its front door was then the Leicester-Huntingdon road (which turned north at Kettering: there was no western extension until the A1-M1 link, today's A14, was built in 1994); and although it was surely too small to service the scheduled stagecoaches and mails whose main stops were at Kettering and Brampton, as one of the innumerable posthouses that lined such roads the George must have sold refreshment both solid and liquid to plenty of private carriages and post-chaises, as well as hiring out (and shoeing) fresh horses.

There hasn't been much east-west through traffic along the High Street for many a year; and even as Spaldwick has relaxed into deep rural tranquillity, so the George has been mutated from bustling waystation to thriving village local, albeit a very upmarket one. The elegant 60-cover restaurant in a former cartshed, and a French and Mediterranean-inspired fine dining menu with mains

AT A GLANCE
Opening times: 12-11 Sun-Thurs; 12-12 Fri-Sat. Food service: 12-2.30, 6-9.30. Car park. Garden. Smoking shelter. Children welcome. **Wheelchair access/ disabled toilet**.

ranging from £10.95 to £19.95, show where the core of the business lies. But the bar, for all its subtly-coloured walls, its stripped floorboards, its sofas and armchairs, and its unusual engraved wooden panels, is still a proper bar, with a choice of real ales (Greene King IPA, Adnams Broadside, and a changing guest), with a bar menu starting at £4.95, with live bands on the last Friday of every month, with home-made pies at £5.95 every Tuesday night, and with a quiz every Sunday. All right, so the nibbles on quiz nights are tapas rather than roasties and Yorkshire puds; but the spirit is there.

Swavesey

White Horse
Market St CB24 4QG
Tel 01954 232470

Occupying pride of place on the corner of Swavesey's old market place, the White Horse has been a prosperous and bustling village inn since at least the reign of George I (whose emblem the white horse was). It may even be much older than that, since the market got its charter in 1244; but the present building dates to shortly after a disastrous fire in 1719, when houses worth £1,755 were de-

stroyed, and is on record in 1765 as one of the town's three inns.

Although not a self-consciously olde-worlde pub, the White Horse is something of a timewarp in that it retains totally separate public and lounge bars with completely different styles of decoration and different clienteles. The public bar has its exposed beams (some of them genuine!), a big brick fireplace, red quarry-tile floor, and scrubbed pine tables. The lounge is smarter and softer, with red carpets and upholstery, sepia photographs of old Swavesey, and a little dining area at the back with somewhat incongruous electric blue chairs. The only bit of tradition missing is higher prices in the lounge.

But its adherence to tradition doesn't make the White Horse sleepy. On the contrary, it's a hive of entertainment with satellite TV, bar billiards and pool – a rare double! – frequent live music, darts of course, and an unusual pinball machine. In fact it's something of a Mecca for pinball – it hosts the South-East of England championship tournament every year, when 14 tables are set up in the pool room.

A favourite with ale lovers – in fact it's the Cambridge branch of CAMRA's reigning Pub of the Year – the White Horse has three changing cask beers, one of them always a golden ale such as Caledonian Deuchar's IPA or Woodforde's Wherry, and a beer festival every May bank holiday weekend.

Waresley

Duncombe Arms
SG19 3BS Tel 01767 650265

The first thing you notice about the white-painted Duncombe Arms is the big porch with its oddly-shaped rounded gable. There's another, almost identical, porch and gable at the side bearing the date 1906; and as the neighbouring cottages with their picture-postcard thatched roofs are clearly estate houses of about the same date you might be excused for thinking that the pub was an Edwardian new-build – perhaps a gift to their tenants from the Duncombes, lords of the manor since the mid-19th century. Not the case, though: a Susan Wilson is recorded as brewing here between 1897 and 1903, so the pub clearly predates a somewhat sub-Lutyens remodelling that includes Tudor-style chimneys.

Inside, the Duncombe Arms is spacious, light, airy and sunny. It's fully carpeted and upholstered for comfort, with little armchairs scattered among the stools and settles; and although there are enough fake beams to feed the big fireplace for a week, the pub has no pretensions to the olde-worlde. It's always busy with locals; but its two dining-rooms are popular with customers from a much wider area as well.

AT A GLANCE
Opening times: 11.30-3, 6-11 Mon-Sat; 12-3, 7-10.30 Sun. Food service: 12-2, 7-9.30 Mon-Sat, 12-2, 7-9 Sun. Mains: £6.95-£14.95. Real ales from Greene King. Car parks front and rear. Big garden. Children in dining rooms only. No dogs.

Wistow

Three Horsehoes
Mill Rd PE28 2QQ Tel 01487 822270

A real traditional village local, the Three Horseshoes is a no-frills pub with something for pretty much everyone. For the beer buff there's well-kept Adnams Bitter and Broadside; for those in search or more solid sustenance there's a wide-ranging and well-priced menu; for anyone who's simply at a loose end there's a big cheerful fireplace to relax beside, plenty of comfy soft seating to relax in, and a good crowd of regulars to relax with. And so it has been for... well, who knows how long?

The deeds only go back to 1862 and show that as well as the pub there was the village blacksmith's forge on the site. But the brick-built, L-shaped main building with its odd-looking hipped gable (which helped the thatched roof shrug off the rain more quickly and efficiently) looks 18th century at least and possibly goes back to the late 17th century when brick began to replace timber-framing as the favoured construction medium in these parts. Blacksmiths often used to brew and sell beer as a sideline, and there's a comic 17th-century ballad on the subject. So it's pleasing to think that the people of Wistow were supping their ale here, just as they do now, 300 years ago.

AT A GLANCE
Opening times: 12-3, 6-11 Mon-Fri; 12-11 Sat; 12-4 Sun. Food service: 12-2, 6-8 Mon-Sat; 12-2 Sun. Sandwiches £3.50-£4.50. mains £7.50-£10. Sky TV. Pool and darts. Car park. Big garden with smoking shelter. Children welcome.

The Brewery Gardens and Visitors Centre are open to the public from 28th April 2009 to 24th September 2009.

Opening hours are 11.30am to 4.30pm
on Tuesday, Wednesday and Thursday each week.

*In addition to the above schedule, our Visitors Centre will also
be open on the following dates:-*
Sunday 7th June, Sunday 5th July and Sunday 2nd August 2009,
from 1.00pm to 4.30pm

North Brink Brewery
Wisbech, Cambs
PE13 1LN
Tel: 01945 583160

info@elgoods-brewery.co.uk • www.elgoods-brewery.co.uk

Breweries in Cambridgeshire

Elgood's

Given the number of pubs it owns in the county, you might be forgiven for thinking that Greene King was Cambridgeshire's premier brewery. Actually, though, it's based in Suffolk, so the honourable position of senior brewery belongs to Elgood's of Wisbech, founded in 1795 and owned by the Elgood family since 1878.

With its 42 pubs mostly clustered within a few miles of Wisbech, Elgood's is among the smallest of Britain's dwindling band of old-established family-owned breweries. But its beers are well worth seeking out, with both Golden Newt and Black Dog constantly winning new medals and certificates. A new range has been added to the portfolio this year to counteract all the recession-related doom and gloom: the Feelgood Factor series kicked off with a chocolate-flavoured version at 3.7% ABV in March, and a fruit-flavoured variant should be with us this summer.

The elegant Georgian brewery itself is well worth a visit and is one of two attractions on North Brink, the other being the National Trust-owned Peckover House. There's a shop and visitor centre (open 11.30-4.30 May-Sept), and the Elgood family has also decided to throw open its breathtakingly beautiful gardens, now recovering nicely from the devastating hurricane of 2007 and a must for all lovers of roses.

Beers: Black Dog Mild 3.6%; Cambridge Bitter 3.8%; Golden Newt 4.1%; Greyhound 5.2%.
North Brink, Wisbech PE13 1LN. Tel 01945 583160. info@elgoods-brewery.co.uk www.elgoods-brewery.co.uk

Cambridge Moonshine

Mark Watch had been a printing company manager for 27 years when, in 2003, the redundancy cheque arrived. But he was also an avid home brewer,

and during the course of a boozy evening with friends – over his own home brew, of course – somehow became convinced it would be a good move to turn his hobby into his living.

Next morning it still seemed like a good idea; a year later Cambridge Moonshine was up and running in Mark's garage. Fortunately for all concerned it was indeed a good idea: Mark's first brew, Mulberry Whale Bitter, was produced for the D Day-themed 2004 Cambridge Beer Festival (the Mulberries were the artificial harbours used after the initial landings) where it won the Beer of the Festival award.

Two years later things were going so well that the brewery had spread from the garage into the shed and every scrap of spare space in Mark's house, and had to be moved into old farm buildings at the top of the Gog Magog Hills. The next highest point eastward is the Ural Mountains; so if you're visiting, don't forget your thermals!

Beers: Harvest Moon Mild 3.8%; Mulberry Whale Bitter 4%; Red Watch Blueberry Ale 4.4%; Black Hole Stout 4.5%; Pigs Ear Porter 4.7%.
28 Radegund Rd, Cambridge CB1 3RS. Tel 07906 066794 mark.watch@ntl-world.com

City of Cambridge

Steve Draper, who founded City of Cambridge Brewery in 1997, is one of the most experienced men on the county's microbrewing scene having previously worked for Bass, Greene King, Carlsberg, and Eldridge Pope.

The brewery was originally located

on Newmarket Road in Cambridge but was forced to move when the site was redeveloped (it's now a Tesco). The new site had no mains drainage, so Steve installed an environmentally-friendly reedbed to process the brewery's waste water. This has won awards for its green credentials and is home to rare species including water voles and reed warblers. Unfortunately you can't visit because with the A10 thundering past the gates Steve's planning permission doesn't allow it. You can, however, sample his superb beers, including the outstanding Hobson's Choice, at gastropubs such as the Anchor at Sutton Gault and the Three Horseshoes at Madingley.

Beers: Jet Black 3.6%; Boathouse Bitter 3.7%; Hobson's Choice 4.1%; Atom Splitter 4.7%; Parkers Porter 5.3%.
Ely Rd, Chittering CB5 9BH. Tel 01223 864864. sales@cambridge-brewery.co.uk www.cambridge-brewery.co.uk

Devil's Dyke

Reach's last pub closed, as did so many other village inns, in the late 1960s. But a public-spirited citizen decided Reach needed a pub, and in 1975 converted his own house into the King's. By 1998 this too faced closure. But they're a stubborn lot in Reach and decided that life without a pub would be intolerable; so they clubbed together to buy it.

In 2003 the villagers leased their pub to Liverpudlian Frank Feehan whose brother Martin was just taking over the Union Inn in Rye, Sussex. A couple of years later Martin decided a pub career was not for him, left the Union, and joined the Metropolitan Police. However he still had a hankering to be involved with the pub trade, so after a while he started brewing beer for Frank's pub. It was a hobby, really – he was only brewing 36-pint batches in the pub kitchen – but these things grow on you, and in 2007 he bought a 2-barrel plant to

install in a barn. It's still only a hobby, though, for Martin is still a full-time policeman. Only when he's not visiting the vengeance of the law on miscreants does he get a chance to roll up his sleeves and mash in a brew, so his beers are only on sale at the pub itself and at local CAMRA beer festivals.

Beers: Bitter 3.8%; No 7 Pale Ale 4.1%; Victorian 4.7%; Strong Mild 5%.
Dyke's End,, 8 Fair Green, Reach CB25 0JD. Tel 01638 743816.

Hereward

Michael Czarnobaj is a freelance management accountant, TV and film extra, local historian, and folk music enthusiast who also loves his real ale and has been to every Cambridge Beer Festival since 1979!

In the late 1990s Michael started brewing for himself in his garage, mainly because he had always loved dark ales and was finding them harder and harder to come by. By 2003 he had decided that Ely deserved its own brewery and, after attending a brewing course, turned his tiny plant into a nearly commercial concern.

I say "nearly" because Hereward is still very much part-time and mainly supplies local beer festivals, shutting up shop completely from May to September. The beers are worth finding, though, not least because of their local links: St Etheldreda founded the abbey in 673AD that later became Ely Cathedral; while Porta Porter is named after the cathedral's south gate which for a brief period in the mid-19th century was home to a small brewery.

Beers: Bitter 3.8%; St Etheldreda's Golden Bitter 4%; Porta Porter 4.2%; Oatmeal Stout 4.5%.
50 Fleetwood, Ely CB6 1BH. Tel 01353 666441. michael.czarnobaj@ntlworld. com

Milton

To hear Richard Naseby tell how he became a brewer, you'd think he just sort of wandered into the business by chance. "I ran the Oxford University Beer Appreciation Society and then when I graduated I did a bit of travel writing," he says. "After a while I thought about getting a proper job but decided against and started Milton Brewery instead."

He's not quite as casual as that, though: you can tell that from the way the brewery has flourished since he founded it in 1999. Not only are his beers on sale in three of Cambridge's top free houses – the St Radegund, the Cambridge Blue, and the Kingston Arms – they're also on sale at the Chop House restaurant in King's Parade and in most of the city's 32 student bars. On top of that the brewery runs four pubs of its own: two in London, one in Norwich, and the Coalheaver's Arms in Peterborough.

As for the classical theme behind the names of the beers, Richard explains: "There were only two possible sources of inspiration, the classical poet John Milton or Milton Fluid, which you use for sterilising baby's bottles. Guess which we went for!"

Beers: Minotaur 3.3%; Jupiter 3.5%; Neptune 3.8%; Pegasus 4.1%; Sparta 4.3%; Nero 5%; Cyclops 5.3%.
111 Cambridge Rd, Milton CB4 6AT. Tel 01223 226198. enquiries@miltonbrewery.co.uk www.miltonbrewery.co.uk

Oakham Ales

As its name suggests, the brewery was originally set up in Oakham, Rutland, in 1993. After five years, though, the founder sold it to Peterborough businessman Paul Hook, who already owned the spectacular Charters Bar, a converted Dutch grainbarge moored in the River Nene.

The brewery promptly moved to a new home in Peterborough's old dole office, a big 1930s building in Westgate which was converted into an enormous pub with a mezzanine floor, superb Thai cuisine, and the brewing equipment proudly displayed behind a glass wall. However the pub, the Brewery Tap, was almost instantly blighted by a Compulsory Purchase Order allowing for its demolition to make way for an extension to the Westgate Shopping Centre. The order has not yet been executed and the Brewery Tap is still trading, with brewing equipment still in situ, but Oakham's main brewery has been moved to bigger premises on the edge of town.

Oakham Ales was a success right from the start owing to the skill and imagination of brewer John Bryant, who is equally at home with very hoppy golden ales and strong dark beers. JHB or Jeffrey Hudson's Bitter, named after a 17th-century court dwarf who was a native of Peterborough, is a former Champion Beer of Britain, while John's dangerously strong winter seasonal, Attila, this year won CAMRA's Winter Beer of Britain competition.

Beers: JHB 3.8%; Inferno 4%; White Dwarf 4.3%; Bishop's Farewell 4.6%.
2 Maxwell Rd, Woodston, Peterborough PE2 7JB. Tel 01733 370500. info@oakhamales.com
www.oakhamales.com

Oakham Ales

Son of Sid

Installing a brewery at one end of the lounge bar "just seemed like a natural progression" to Bob Mitchell, who had been serving a huge variety of real ales to the villagers of the Gransdens since he took over the Chequers from his dad Sid in 1993.

And Bob's a big believer in variety. For although he only produces one regular ale, he had brewed more than 40 limited edition specials within 18 months of installing the brewery – you can see it through the lounge bar window – in 2007. And as well as his own beers, Bob also stocks a wide range from other microbreweries. "There's an awful lot of good beers out there, and a bit of variety does you good," he says.

It's hard work, mind: Bob only brews once a week, but reckons the business keeps him busy for three days a week; and on top of that he's got a thriving pub to run. "It's a bit like Hotel California," he says. "You can never really leave!"

To sample Bob's ales you'll have to travel to Little Gransden, because he only brews for the pub and local beer festivals. And you won't be the only one. "Trade's definitely gone up since I opened the brewery, so it's been well worth the effort!" he says.

Beers: First Brew 4.6%.
The Chequers, Little Gransden SG19 3DW. Tel 01767 677348. chequers-gransden@btinternet.com

Tydd Steam

Will Neaverson was a farmer at Long Sutton in Lincolnshire who also had a passion for home brewing. When his family bought a farm at Tydd St Giles he found it had a derelict barn that would make the ideal brewery – so in summer 2007 he sold his shares in the family business and set up as a brewer instead.

"I'd progressed from using home-brew kits to full-mash brewing, and I was brewing pretty much every weekend," he says. "People liked my beer, so I decided to turn my hobby into my living."

The barn that now houses Will's five-barrel plant was, before the Neaversons bought it, home to two 1900-vintage steam-powered traction engines that had actually been in use right up to the moment of sale – surely the last working steam engines in British agriculture? They are now in retirement at the Museum of Lincolnshire Life, but their memory lives on in the naming of Will's brewery.

Beers: Scoundrel 3.8%; Swedish Blonde 4%; Piston Bitter 4.4%; Mother in Law 4.5%; Piston Bob 4.6%.
Manor Barn, Kirkgate, Tydd St Giles PE13 5NE. Tel 01945 871020. tydd-steam@fsmail.net

Ufford Ales

If you share the current belief in the importance of fresh local produce, you'll be a firm supporter of Ufford Ales. The

Son of Sid

brewery is the joint brainchild of brewer Simon Raines and entrepreneur Michael Thurlby, whose six pubs in and around Stamford are mainly supplied with foodstuffs from his own farm and others in the immediate area.

When Michael bought the White Hart in 2004, it seemed an obvious extension of his philosophy of localism to install a microbrewery in the pub's barn; and although Simon had a day-job as a cleaning supplies sales rep – or perhaps because he had a day-job as a cleaning supplies sales rep! – he volunteered to run it. And so in February 2005 he started giving up his weekends to the task of producing beer for the pubs on a tiny three-barrel plant.

Soon, though, one brew a week wasn't enough; and then two brews a week weren't enough; and when in April 2006 it went up to three brews a week Simon jacked in the day-job and made his hobby his living.

It hasn't stopped there: earlier this year the three-barrel plant (a brewer's barrel is 36 gallons; a half-barrel is a kilderkin and a quarter-barrel is a firkin) was replaced with a 10-barrel plant and plans were also put in hand to install a small bottling line. Half of the output goes to Michael's pubs including the White Hart; the rest is sold to beer festivals and a handful of free houses in the area.

Beers: White Hart 3.8%; Idle Hour 3.9%; Red Clover 4.5%.
White Hart, Main St, Ufford PE9 3BH. Tel 01780 740250. info@ufford-ales.co.uk www.ufford-ales.co.uk

Other breweries well-represented in Cambridgeshire

As well as Cambridgeshire's own flock of breweries, many others are well-represented in the county's pubs.

Chief among them is, of course, the

Ufford Ales

mighty **Greene King,** based just across the Suffolk border in Bury St Edmunds but by far the dominant power in Cambridgeshire. Greene King is a national force to be reckoned with, too: its IPA is Britain's best-selling cask beer; Old Speckled Hen is a nationally-known strong bottled beer; and Greene King also has a formidable presence in Scotland through its ownership of Belhaven of Dunbar.

Pubs belonging to **Charles Wells** of Bedford are to be found in the western parts of the county; and its beers, especially Bombardier, are widely distributed in the free trade. The legendary **Adnams** of Southwold, Suffolk, owns a handful of Cambridgeshire pubs, but its beers, especially Bitter and Broadside, are a common sight here, as is London pride from London brewer **Fuller's**.

Bateman's of Wainfleet, Lincolnshire, now owns three pubs in Cambridgeshire; and of the region's microbrewers both **Nethergate** of Pentlow, Suffolk, and **Woodforde** of Woodbastwick, Norfolk, have loyal followings.

Index by pub name

Nominate a Pub!

Know a great Cambridgeshire pub that isn't in the guide? Then why not do your landlord and landlady a favour and nominate it for the next edition? After all, what better way to select pubs for a guide than by asking the people who really know... the customers?

And while we can't promise that every pub nominated will make the final cut, we can guarantee that every pub nominated will be inspected.

If you'd like to see your local chosen as one of Cambridgeshire's Best Pubs, just send the following details to me, Ted Bruning, at County Life Publishing, 32 Elizabeth Way, Gamlingay, Cambridgeshire SG19 3NH.

- **Name of pub**
- **Name of landlord/landlady**
- **Full postal address including postcode**
- **Telephone number of pub**
- **Web address (if any)**
- **Why the above is one of the Best Pubs in Cambridgeshire (max 100 words)**
- **Your name**
- **Your daytime telephone number**

Get the next edition sent to your home!

To order more copies, or get the next edition sent direct to your home for just £4, simply email your name, address and daytime phone number to sales@bestpubsin. com and we'll get back to you.